BS-WL

D0409286

30109 0 10524281

DIVING FOR THE *GRIFFIN*

DIVING FOR THE

Griffin

Charles Daggett with Kris Shaffer

Weidenfeld and Nicolson · London

Maps by Richard Natkiel Associates

Copyright © Charles Daggett and Christopher Shaffer, 1990

First published in Great Britain by
George Weidenfeld & Nicolson Limited
91 Clapham High Street
London SW4 7TA

All rights reserved. No part of this publication may
be reproduced, stored in a retrieval system, or transmitted,
in any form or by any means, electronic, mechanical,
photocopying, recording or otherwise, without the prior
permission of the copyright owner.

ISBN 0 297 81063 4

Printed in Great Britain by The Bath Press, Avon

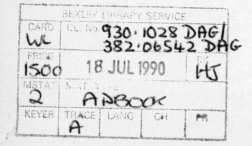

BEXLEY LIBRARY SERVICE				
CARD	CL. No. 930·1028 DAG/			
WL	382·06542 DAG			
PRICE				DK
1500	18 JUL 1990			HJ
MSTAT	MAT TYPE			
2	A BOOK			
KEYER	TRACE	LANG	CH	PR
	A			

DEDICATED

to

LILY SHAFFER

and

CONSTANCE DAGGETT

both of whom were born
during the excavation of the *Griffin*

Contents

════

Illustrations

≡≡≡

Acknowledgements

The vast majority of historical information pertaining to the *Griffin* was gathered at the India Office Library and Records, London, and I must thank all the staff there who, once they realized that this was a serious study, were always keen to help and make suggestions for further avenues of research. Of particular help was Mr Andrew Cook, who has made a fifteen-year study into Alexander Dalrymple's life and also produced, with amazing alacrity, the many charts and pilot books I requested. The Deputy Director, Mr Anthony Farringdon, has done remarkable research into all the ships of the East India Company and very kindly permitted me to study his unpublished work.

I also received great assistance from the staff of all the other libraries I consulted, in particular the London Library, the National Maritime Museum, the British Library, the Bodleian Library, the Guildhall Library and the Public Records Office.

My research on Thomas Dethick and his family was widespread and I would like particularly to record my thanks to Mr Paul Dethick of Sutton-in-Ashford, Notts, who very kindly gave me all of his notes on his family. I searched (unsuccessfully) all over the country to find the date of Captain Dethick's birth and his grave, and in this quest was helped by Mrs Ursula Dickson of Bridgnorth, the Rev Ian Arthur of Sutton, Beds, whose church contains a stained glass window to the memory of Thomas's grandson and last surviving relative, Charles Dethick Blyth; Mr Dudley Fowkes of the Staffordshire Record Office, Mrs Patricia Gill of the West Sussex Record Office, Mrs M. Halford of the Shropshire Record Office, Miss Jill Hanson of the Berkshire Record Office, Mrs Catherine Bowden of the William Salt Library and Mrs Doris Pullen, whom I met at the Society of Genealogists. For other Dethick research, my thanks are due to Professor Donald Coleman and the staff of the Bancroft Library, London.

Mr Eric Gregory of Messrs Thompson Lloyd Ewart Ltd readily answered my questions about tea; the staff of both the Victoria and Albert Museum and the Percival David Foundation were most helpful when dealing with porcelain enquiries, and Patrick Conner of the Martyn Gregory Gallery, 34 Bury Street, London SW1, was a fund of knowledge on China and has also most kindly arranged for me to reproduce a painting which the gallery owned.

In my search for original details concerning the *Griffin*, I should like particularly to thank Mr Charles Burrell, a direct descendant of Sir Charles Raymond, who permitted me to look through his family's private papers. I was introduced to Mr Burrell by Lord Denman, who has helped me over a number of matters, both in London and in the Philippines, where he gave me a very valuable introduction to Mr Jaime Zobell, and I would especially like to record my gratitude to him.

To all the crew of the *China Sea Explorer* I extend my thanks and also to Ian Townley, director of shore operations, who gave me considerable help and hospitality in Manila. Thanks also to Lenora Johanson, who made the film on the *Griffin*'s excavation and arranged most of the photographs I have used, Mark Balsiger, Tim Burrell, Tom Steider, Frederick Osada, Evelyne Jay and Franck Goddio. This book and the expedition would not have been possible without the contribution made by Terry Restall and Kris's brother, Bill Shaffer. In London I was assisted by Lisa Mabbutt and Miranda Arkell.

Finally, my wife Caroline read, re-read and typed several drafts before the final manuscript was ready and made hundreds of suggestions to make this book more readable. To her I extend all my love and thanks.

C.D.
London 1990

CHAPTER 1

---

21 January 1761

The breaking dawn revealed five East Indiamen spread over about a mile of calm sea and at anchor. Six hours earlier a single cannon blast had told the fleet that the leading ship, the *Griffin*, had seen the coast of Mindanao looming out of the moonlit sky about ten miles ahead. Her commander, Captain Dethick, had asked for soundings and, upon learning that there was no ground at thirty-five fathoms, ordered a reduced sail. Sailors, roused from their hammocks, emerged from below and mechanically went through a well-rehearsed drill and, before long, the ship had slowed down and was tacking against the slight headwind on a south-westerly course. As they approached, the land began to curve around to the west and the Captain ordered a change in course to avoid coming too close to shore before deciding to haul up until morning. In these uncharted waters there was no point in taking risks, especially when there was a fortune of the Honourable Company's goods on board, not to mention £10,000 worth of his own 'private trade'.

At 6.30 a.m. they were under way again and moved in closer to the land mass in order to follow it southwards. There was now a good breeze coming steadily from the north-east and, although it was hot, the uncomfortable close humidity of the night had lifted. There had been a little rain the previous day, but the ship was basically dry and the crew were happy to be on their way home after more than a year away. Captain Dethick noted these things with satisfaction as he looked around. The damaged mast was now fixed, all the sails and rigging had been repaired in China, the hull had been retarred and caulked and, although the old ship creaked and groaned a little, the *Griffin* was still a good sailer and it was a pleasure to see everything and everyone working well. There was nothing more unpleasant than to be nursing a ship in need of repairs when the sailors were wet through and living off old weavel-infested food and bad water.

From his position in front of the wheel the Captain looked over the main deck, crowded with the livestock which would gradually be killed to provide fresh meat and, turning around, he looked fondly up to the raised platform at the stern. This, the poop deck, was his own private domain and was laden with coops for chickens and ducks and boxes full of green vegetables. Just after the *Griffin* got underway, John Dupree, the Captain's cook had gathered some eggs, milked one of the cows and was now cooking some ham in the small galley adjoining the cuddy, the officers' ward room. Captain Dethick and his Chief Mate, Mr Hudson, breakfasted there and discussed the day's sail. With good luck they would be in 'Soloo' in three days and then on to the Macassar Strait and safety. So far no reefs had been spotted, but everyone saw the sense in keeping a double watch and taking soundings continually around the clock.

Later that morning the *Cuddalore* hove into view and sailed towards the *Griffin*. Captain Dalrymple made the signal to 'talk to the ship' and came over in his longboat for a consultation. Captain Dethick, as the senior commander, was the fleet's Commodore and the other captains received their orders from him. He in turn was forced to take the instructions of Captain Dalrymple, who was commissioned to be their guide through the Philippines, but appeared to be much more interested in making charts. None of them had ever sailed these waters before and there was no pilot book to help, but some years earlier Dalrymple had purchased the library of a private trader who operated between Manila and Madras and, amongst the books, had come across some Portuguese and Spanish sailing instructions, which he was now using. These mentioned two high islands known as the Hare's Ears and the lookouts were instructed to search for them, but the morning haze made visibility poor.

Before lunch Mr Lockwood appeared and joined the Captain on the poop. They had known each other for many years and he had chosen to sail home in the *Griffin* after retiring from a five-year stint as head of the Canton factory. Several weeks earlier, whilst the ship was still moored at Whampoa, the crew had watched with wonder as all his splendid goods were brought on board. On the *Griffin*'s previous voyage to China in 1756, she had picked up James Flint in Bantam and taken him to Ningpo, further up the Chinese coast from Canton. This had been the first stage in a bold undertaking which took him to Peking, the centre of the Chinese Empire, and caused such an uproar in Canton that he had been thrown into prison near Macau for three years. Thomas Lockwood had been at the centre of this scandal and the two men discussed his fate whilst watching the heavily wooded coastline glide past.

The rest of the crew had little to do other than stand by for alterations to the sails. Usually they would be busy stitching canvas, making small repairs and drying out their possessions. Now many of them fished or told stories of devious Chinamen whilst smoking the clay pipes which had been bought from a Swedish ship. Others spoke of fights with rival sailors and various excesses in the drinking shops which sprang up around the Whampoa anchorage each year as soon as the European ships arrived. Those who were not on duty were below decks in the long room towards the bow which was their living and sleeping accommodation. The ports on each side let in a little light, but most of this was effectively blocked by the cannons and the hammocks slung between their carriages. The floor was littered with sailors' individual boxes containing their meagre possessions and on these men sat playing cards, talking, admiring their new tattoos or gingerly examining bruises. Others were asleep in yet more hammocks suspended from the roof. The air was thick with the smell of tobacco and tea. Later this would mingle with the odour of soaking wood and damp clothing, but the voyage was too young for this as yet, even though the crossing from China had been rough.

The officers and midshipmen had various jobs to do, but on the whole there was very little going on. The day's major interest came at around two o'clock, when the beer ration was issued just before dinner time. The Captain kept a good table and, as this was the most important meal of the day, the senior officers, passengers and several favoured young gentlemen who were on their first voyage and whose parents had paid for them to 'learn the sea' all attended. There was still a steady supply of wine, and the party was in excellent spirits as it awaited the arrival of the Captain and his honoured guest, Mr Lockwood. The meal, which was sumptuous for a ship, consisted of soup, then chicken and duck with vegetables and was rounded off with pudding. Afterwards they sat back with a glass of Madeira for a short while until the Captain's departure signaled the end of the meal. Not far away the Third Mate kept his own mess, where the junior officers and midshipmen ate a much less substantial meal. At the bow, in the fo'c'sle, was the crew's cookhouse. Most of their food was boiled; salted pork or beef, fish and, coming from China, rice were the norm, but the *Griffin* was ahead of its time in that there was a baker on board, so the bread and biscuits were fresh and worth eating. Normally ships biscuits were a last resort.

By this time the Hare's Ears were well in sight, two remarkable hills rising to a considerable height from the sea which looked just like a pair of alert ears. The ship was still heading south-west with a good breeze and current to carry her along, but during the late afternoon the course was changed slightly to west-south-west in order to take the *Griffin* further away from the coast which was again curving to the west. By sunset she was off the southernmost part of the island, about fifteen miles to the east. The Hare's Ears were south-west a similar distance away and, as another island appeared to be closer but in the same direction, the Captain gave the order to haul up.

The other Indiamen, all sailing a similar course behind the *Griffin*, saw her signal and also slowed down. Her longboat was lowered and the Second Mate, David Saunders, was rowed over to the *Pocock*, the nearest of the four, to tell her to keep the islands well to the larboard (left) and to haul up for the night just after 10.30. The boat then returned and in turn *Pocock*'s longboat was sent off to the next ship and so on until the message had passed through the little fleet.

For most of the day the *Cuddalore* had been a long way in front and she appeared to be setting a course to pass by the Hare's Ears on her starboard side, but Captain Dethick was taking no chances as Dalrymple, whom he regarded as a very odd character, could sail through much shallower water.

Passing the instructions took a while and the *Griffin* was well under way by the time the last ship received the message, so they were now even further apart. At 8 p.m., half an hour after sunset, there was still enough light for visibility to be no problem, although the slackening breeze once again made the humidity more oppressive. Mr Lockwood had retired to his cabin, but the Captain and First Mate were on deck with their telescopes looking for any tell-tale white topped waves which might signal a reef and taking sightings with their octants. At the bow the seamen took soundings and two kept watch from the top of the main mast. The Second Mate stood at the base of the ladder which led up to the poop ready to pass on any orders from the Captain to the helmsman and the other officers were gathered further forward giving the midshipmen instruction in taking sightings at night. On the horizon, at south-east, a low black mass indicated another island; the height made it difficult to judge the distance, but it appeared to be about ten miles away. The *Cuddalore* had disappeared.

An hour later, as low tide came, the current was much stronger and the southern part of the Hare's Ears was due east. The low flat island was still south-east a safe distance away and, before retiring to his cabin, the Captain told the officer of the watch to continue steering west-south-west.

Unbeknownst to Captain Dethick, the glassy surface of the sea disguised an undercurrent running at over five knots about ten degrees off due south and the wind had dropped so much that the ship was being pulled with the current to the extent that she was heading almost sixty degrees further to the south than they thought. The low flat island which had been south-east actually has another slightly higher one about two miles behind it on the *Griffin*'s blind side, which, in the moonlight, appeared to merge with the first one and the lookouts in the crow's nest were becoming confused as to exactly what they were seeing. Just after 10.30 p.m. it appeared to be a safe eight miles away. It was less than five.

Fifteen minutes later the order was given to haul up for the night. The low island suddenly looked uncomfortably close, only about three miles to the east-south-east and nearer still were rips which an inexperienced officer might have thought were caused by the rushing tide. In fact this was a reef which extended $2\frac{3}{4}$ miles from the island and was now only a few feet underwater. The ship's wheel was brought sharply around to turn her into the wind and, as she moved about, the calm evening was destroyed by a loud thud from down below. With it came a jarring shock which reverberated throughout the ship and then, immediately afterwards, a terrible grinding sound brought the vessel to a halt. In his cabin, the Captain was dictating his log notes to Thomas Hodgson, his clerk. He knew in an instant that his ship had struck something and rushed out past the wheel and into the open air.

Everywhere he saw confusion. The ship had stopped dead and sailors hung over the sides frantically scanning the water for evidence of a reef. The cows and other animals, sensing the tension, were all making a great noise and his own coops obscured the view from vital parts of the poop. Panic had not yet set in and down on the main deck the other officers were looking up for guidance. As all men in command feel when faced with a decision affecting the lives of their men, Thomas Dethick experienced the sudden sensation of being completely alone but, nothing if not an experienced sailor, he braced himself and quickly shouted his orders, 'Haul down the sails. Mr Armourer, kindly sound the cannons. And Mr Saunders to light fires at the bow, if you please.'

Once these were given out at least the crew would have something to do and the other ships would be warned. Dethick turned to his Chief Mate and lifelong friend, Charles Hudson, and told him to take a number of sailors down into the bilges to see what damage had been sustained. Hudson went off at a run and, after he disap-

peared, the Captain turned to a shocked and nervous Thomas Lockwood to tell him there was no cause for alarm, the ship would be
off the reef in a few minutes.

It was fifteen minutes before the first guns went off. The other
ships fortunately recognized the danger signals and immediately
hauled up. Each of them sounded and found ten or less fathoms
before sending their largest anchors crashing into the water. The
tide was drawing them towards the reef and both the *Valentine* and
Oxford snapped their anchor chains on taking up the tension, so they
desperately set a course to the north-west and out of danger. The
Suffolk was further astern and also turned away, and only the *Pocock*
was able to hold fast about two miles from the stricken *Griffin*. All
of them lowered longboats and the sea, despite the tide, was strangely
calm so they had no trouble rowing, but the first did not arrive until
midnight, an hour later.

During this time, the *Griffin* had been pulled over the reef by the
sheer strength of the current and Dethick had dropped his anchors
to try and hold her. Charles Hudson took about half an hour to
return to the poop deck. His report was not good. Whilst inspecting
the damage, the ship had begun to move and the holes, previously
blocked by rocks were now exposed to the rush of water. The seamen
were sent to the pumps and reported them to be not operating properly. Hudson cursed the lack of maintenance, but ordered the men
to keep going. By the time he left there was six feet of water in
the well; three more would be virtually fatal.

Dethick could see that the only chance he had was to try and beach
his ship. He ordered the longboat and pinnace overboard and threw
ropes to them. Emergency sails were set and the helmsman was told
to set course for the island. Everything ready, he ordered the anchor
chains to be cut and told the rowers to pull with everything they
had. Almost immediately, the ship groaned and began to edge forward but, within minutes there was another dreadful jolt and again
she ground to a halt. Now the only recourse was to lighten the ship.
Everybody still on board pushed and heaved against the cannons
and they slowly smashed through the ports and overboard. Dethick
watched this and told Mr Lockwood and his other passenger, Dr
Herriot, to make preparations for abandoning ship. There was still
a chance of saving her if the load could be lightened enough to keep
afloat until high tide, but it was wiser to have these two away to
safety and the nearest longboat was only a few minutes away. It
came alongside, and Lockwood and Herriot together with their servants, laden with what few precious possessions they had managed

to gather, clambered aboard. They arrived at the *Pocock* at 1.30, full of tales of woe.

It was a relief to see them off and the Captain made his way through the human chain of men passing tables, chairs, barrels and all other movable objects and throwing them overboard. He descended into the lowest deck, immediately above the hold. Here the chain pumps were by this time covered with water, which was rapidly rising. The well was twelve feet deep and he knew that once water overflowed on to the deck, the ship was doomed, though he hoped she was a couple of feet higher now that the cannons had gone. Once again on deck, he peered down to the inky black water: there was no change. Everything had gone and the sailors looked around hope-lessly. The safety of the beach was too far away and Dethick could see another longboat approaching. He knew the crew's safety was paramount and told those already in the boats to push off.

At 3.30 a.m. the *Pocock*'s boat and pinnace pulled up and her officer came on board. There were by now only twenty sailors and the two most senior officers left. The steering gear and rudder were inoper-able, and the wallowing *Griffin*, completely out of control, began to drift further south with the tide. The *Oxford*'s boat also came along-side after a three-hour row and, as she did so, water bubbled up through the hatches on the main deck and began to lap against the waist boards. Captain Dethick ordered all the others to leave before sadly turning towards his cabin to collect the ship's log book and secret instructions. Charles Hudson waited and was gratified to see him come out a few minutes later. He paused to survey what was left of the ship he had commanded for twelve years before climbing into the *Oxford*'s boat. They stood off for a little while until the *Griffin* sank and then began the long pull to the nearest ship. It was almost dawn. Thomas Dethick stood in the stern and silently cursed Alex-ander Dalrymple.

CHAPTER 2

≡≡≡

The East India Company in China

'The China Trade has . . . become one of the principle objects of the Company's attention.'
Court of Directors to Fort William (Calcutta),
1 November 1758

'It is of very small consequence to this country.'
Tsontock (Viceroy) of Canton to English factors,
30 September 1760

1760

For the past five years the English merchants, or supracargoes as they were universally known, had been permitted to remain in Canton after the ships departed each January and this had dramatically improved the quality of their otherwise extremely difficult lives. Before, when they had arrived with the ships during June or July, there had been a frantic rush from the anchorage at Whampoa to the city, some ten miles down river, to place their orders for the season's goods with the Chinese shopkeepers or *hongists* before their European rivals took all the best tea, and to rent a factory before the ships began to unload. Now they had a reasonable routine and were able to bargain properly and leisurely with the *hongists* during the spring and ensure that the best quality tea and chinaware was purchased. There was also more time in which to dispose of the English cloth the Indiamen brought, so the new arrangement whereby three supracargoes remained every year as what was called the 'Resident Council' worked very well.

1760 did not even begin as it should have. To start with, a large number of Indiamen had arrived unexpectedly at Whampoa in 1759 and their orders from the *hongists* were not sufficient to fulfil the requirements, so more tea had to be bought at inflated 'late season' prices and this was still being delivered in January. The last three

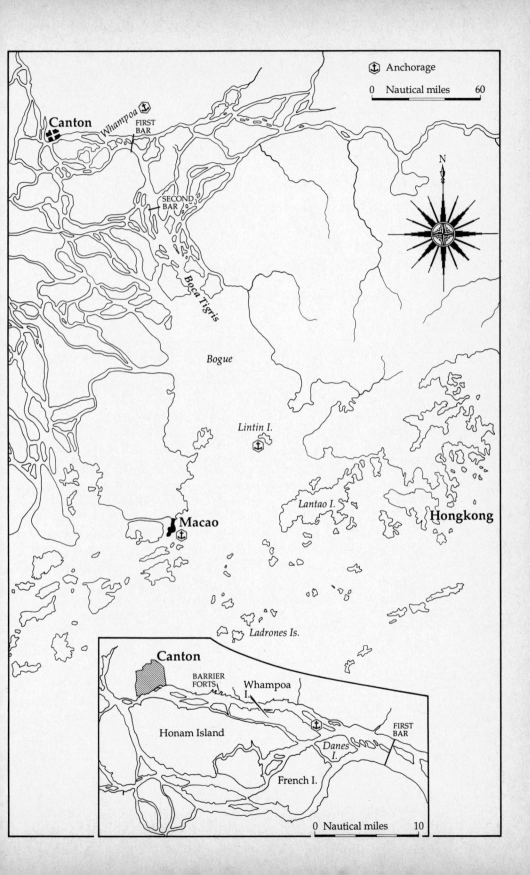

Anchorage

0   Nautical miles   60

N

Canton
Whampoa
FIRST
BAR

SECOND
BAR

Boca Tigris

Bogue

Lintin I.

Lantao I.

Macao

Hongkong

Ladrones Is.

Canton

BARRIER
FORTS

Whampoa
I.

Honam Island

Danes
I.

FIRST
BAR

French I.

0 Nautical miles 10

ships had finally departed on 7 February, and it was fortunate that the monsoon had not yet changed.*

The three men who formed this year's Resident Council, Thomas Lockwood, Francis Kinnersley (who had sailed on the *Griffin*'s maiden voyage in 1749) and Francis Wood, were all experienced supracargoes and looked forward to a well-earned break before the annual round of bargaining for the next season began. However, no sooner had they cleared the factory† (a long, narrow building they rented from the *hongists* and which doubled as their living accommodation and warehouse or trading base), than a letter came from Alexander Dalrymple, who had first appeared at Macau in July 1759 asking for provisions, which they had not been able to supply. He had been there almost ever since.

Dalrymple now related a long and tedious story about how some men from his ship, the *Cuddalore*, had been imprisoned by the Portuguese for riotous behaviour. This in itself did not seem to be serious – similar incidents happened at Whampoa almost every year – but the Portuguese led a precarious existence in Macau in constant fear of irritating the Chinese, and Dalrymple's men appeared to have drunkenly attacked some of them. The next day it seemed that more men were locked up and Dalrymple had formed the opinion that England and Portugal were suddenly at war. He sent a 'flag of truce' to the shore together with a letter enquiring what was going on, to which the Governor replied asking that the letter be rewritten in Portuguese or French, as he did not understand English. Dalrymple, instead of coming up to Canton as he ought, replied that the English 'thought it beneath them to write in any other language' and the affair degenerated. There were more arrests and the Governor threatened to set the *Cuddalore* on fire. As all the supracargoes could speak Portuguese, they made the long trip down to Macau and appeased the authorities with assurances to the Chinese that no offence to them was intended.

No sooner were they back at Canton than a messenger brought a letter from James Flint, written from his prison cell, asking for 800 taels (the Chinese tael was converted at three to the pound sterling) and saying, 'I hope you will not show the least backwardness . . . for I shall suffer for it if it is not fulfilled.'

Flint had been sent to China by the East India Company in 1736

* The north-east monsoon would carry a ship towards the Malacca Strait, but it changed direction around the beginning of February and a ship which was too late leaving would have to spend another year in Whampoa.
† The merchants who accompanied the ships on these early voyages were called factors, so a factory is literally a place for factors.

to learn the language as there was a suspicion that the official 'linguists' or translators did not always repeat everything that was said. He proved to be a great asset to the supracargoes and, two years previously, had been sent up the coast to try and discover why the ports of Chusan and Limpo had suddenly been closed, leaving only Canton open for foreign trade. He had actually made his way to Peking and managed to attract the authorities' attention to his complaint by having a large placard made on which was printed his petition. A senior official was appointed to return with him to Canton to investigate and, in the ensuing inquiry, the *Hoppo,* the most senior customs official, had been convicted of corruption and dismissed. The supracargoes had rejoiced at the drop in taxes but, as soon as the investigator returned to Peking, they were invited to the *Tsontock's* (Viceroy) palace inside the forbidden walled city. They rode in covered chairs through one of the three gates and, Lockwood noted, when the audience began, 'he then gave the order for Mr Flint to advance towards him, [and] he pointed to a writing which he said was the Emperor's edict for Mr Flint's banishment to Macau for three years and then to return to England, never more to come into this country.' The Chinese linguist who had written the petition also came forward and was informed that he was to be beheaded.

The 'Emperor's edict' was patently a fake, but this was the first time the Chinese had arrested an Englishman and it gave the supracargoes an insight into just how determined the officials were that no foreigners should attempt to meddle in their affairs. Flint's messenger was given the money and it was hoped that his life would be made more bearable. The 'loan' that his prison governor had requested was no more than naming the price of his bribe, but in a country where nothing happened without such payments at least this method was preferable to insulting him by offering too little.

Whilst these irritating problems were being dealt with, the *hongists* who usually came to the factory were conspicuous by their absence and it was feared that 'they are forming themselves into an association' to fix the price of tea. The Chinese authorities only permitted the supracargoes to do business with a small number of officially designated *hongists* and, so far, this had worked relatively well as those who were appointed were the most established in Canton and least likely to go bankrupt, a regular occurrence among the smaller merchants. It was infuriating to know that tea could be bought more cheaply from merchants on the outskirts of Canton; some advances had been made to them and letters were also sent to tea producing areas in an effort to buy directly at source. The possibility that the only people who were permitted to deal with the Europeans were preparing to fix the price of tea was utterly horrifying as the trade could be completely killed by too much greed. Thus the supracargoes decided to make no contracts whatsoever until the position was clear.

On 12 April they heard that the *hongists* had held another meeting, but this news was overshadowed by a series of new regulations which the *Tsontock* claimed had come from the Emperor:

1. The supracargoes must leave Canton when the ships departed and there would be a fixed time for them to remain in China. If any business was unfinished, they could go to Macau and remain there.
2. The *hongists* would be held responsible for the wrongdoings of any foreigner.
3. Lending money to any *hongist* was prohibited on penalty of confiscation of all the lender's property.
4. It was forbidden for any Chinese to carry letters on a European's behalf.
5. The ships and people at Whampoa would be guarded by soldiers as many foreigners 'are of a wild and brutish nature and may easily occasion trouble'.

These new restrictions were almost certainly a further penalty for Flint's actions and were each directed at damaging an aspect of trade. If the supracargoes were again forced to sail with their ships, future orders could not be properly placed unless the *hongists*, who operated on almost no capital of their own, were advanced money to purchase the goods. If an advance was seen to be a loan, which it could be if the officials decided it was, then this would mean that trade would grind to a halt. The prohibition against Chinese carrying letters destroyed any hope of finding cheaper suppliers, and the *hongists* being responsible for 'wrongdoings' was open to such wide interpretation as to guarantee that this could be used for almost anything. Soldiers guarding the sailors would certainly incite more rioting and the convention of the Chinese agreeing to extraterritoriality or the use of English law for Englishmen could be in jeopardy.

Several days later they called a sympathetic *hongist* named Chetqua to the factory and told him that they would give large orders to him and two others if the association was disbanded. He promised to consider the offer. Whilst they were waiting for an answer, first Dalrymple complained about a new insult and then the linguists and other servants were all 'thrown into chains' because the Europeans had not departed.

Time was running out and, on 1 May, they were still resisting the *hongists'* prices, saying they were too high, but four days later Lockwood decided 'that we cannot possibly expect to engage upon more favourable terms ... and the season being so advanced, we sent for the merchants and entered into contracts with them'. On 10 May the three supracargoes closed the factory, paid the *hongists* in advance and took a boat down river to Macau, baffled and disillusioned over the inexplicable downturn in the relations with the Chinese officials and defeated by the 'co-hong' of merchants.

The Chinese, however, would have been amazed had they known of the Englishmen's dissatisfaction. As far as they were concerned, it was a great concession that the 'foreign devils' should be permitted to trade in China at all and they should always remain grateful, no matter what conditions were attached to the privilege. Chinese history from the earliest times taught that theirs was an ideal society to which everyone else should aspire. In over 1,000 years of glorious Chinese civilization there had been only one unfortunate incident when, in the thirteenth century, the Mongol hoards had swept down from the north and their leader, Kublai Khan, became China's Emperor. He ousted the Chinese officials from their positions and encouraged trade with foreigners, but fortunately from the point of view of contemporary teaching, after a century of his repression, peasants from the centre of China rebelled and, following a great struggle, expelled the hated regime and began a new dynasty, that of the Mings.

With them came xenophobia and a strengthening of Confucian ideology, which was combined with a concept of China being the centre of the Earth, if not the universe. After only a couple of generations all contact with the outside world was abandoned and the Ming Emperor declared himself to be the Son of Heaven. The capital, Peking, became the centre of all things desirable, a type of harmonious balance between Heaven and Earth, and, as it was believed that the Earth had a type of 'life force' which flowed through it like blood through veins, all buildings were carefully constructed to benefit from this 'force'. Under the Mings, China gloried in her isolation, a completely self-sufficient country whose people believed that anything and everything outside their borders was quite uninteresting and unattractive.

Initially the Mings had continued the policy of the previous dynasty in sending large fleets of huge junks, at least five times the size of the largest vessel in Europe, on expeditions to India and as far as Africa, but in 1644 these were banned, the junks dismantled and a new set of beliefs heralded China's withdrawal into herself. The official explanation for calling a halt to sea journeys was that, if Chinese people settled in foreign lands (which they were doing, forming merchant enclaves), there would be a great drain on the economy due to the fact that outside China there was nothing to eat except wild animals and nothing to make cloth out of, so the Son of Heaven would have to send rice and clothing to his subjects abroad. The real reason was that Arab traders had no need to come with their silver to China if the Chinese went to them, so the fact that sea voyages represented a drain on the economy was true, but the feeling went further than that as the Emperor did not want to have any contact with the outside world. The Mings constructed a great system of inland waterways which was so extensive that goods could move from north to south without travelling by sea at all. It was intimated that anyone carrying goods on the sea was trying to avoid paying taxes and this, combined with an increasing number of Japanese pirates (the 'dwarf robbers'), made coastal regions the least desirable part of the Central Flowery Kingdom.

It was decided that all lands outside China were uncivilized and populated by tribal barbarians. Those people with whom China had some contact, by virtue of their living in border regions, were considered to be barbarians who were aware of their lack of civilization and, in this enlightened state, were permitted to send envoys who could learn something of the Chinese system and take their knowledge home in an attempt to improve themselves. The Emperor decreed that these ambassadors were to be treated well and provided with proper clothes and food whilst being escorted to the capital to give their crude gifts. Once in Peking, the Emperor, great in his magnanimity, might accord them the unspeakable honour of an audience. This happened at dawn when, in a chamber called the Hall of the Blending of Heaven and Earth Inside the Great Within, the Emperor sat upon his throne and was illuminated by the first rays of the sun. As soon as this happened the foreigners prostrated themselves on the ground and touched their heads on the floor nine times before rapidly retiring to a magnificent breakfast. This was the famous ceremony of the *kowtow*. A few days later the foreigner would receive a letter from the Emperor and, duly inspired, would then depart.

Confucianism in China taught a highly traditionalist set of values and the civil service was chosen from those who passed formidable examinations in the philosopher's teachings. Passing the first test, which required at least six years' study, gave a candidate status in society and three more tests were available for successive promotion to higher grades. Society considered farmers and scholar-officials to be the most honourable groups as they were seen to be working selflessly for the good of the people while merchants were placed at the bottom of the social tree. Commerce was regarded as one of the lowest forms of human endeavour because, according to the four-teenth-century writer Wang Chen, it was 'manipulating surpluses' and commerce from across the sea was the lowest of the low. Mer-chants' sons were precluded from sitting the Imperial examinations and the only way a rich trader could gain any respectability was to give up his business and purchase a farming estate, in much the same way as a British merchant would achieve gentility two centuries later. The officials were the only ones who were able to give their children enough education to pass the examinations, so the system, rather than being a pure meritocracy as was intended, became an oligarchy and extremely conservative.

Confucius taught five virtues: benevolence, righteousness, pro-priety, wisdom and trustworthiness, and placed absolute emphasis on the family unit. Another doctrine, Taoism, was taught in conjunc-tion with that of Confucius and this propounded the belief that the basis of civilization was an inner harmony of the soul. It encouraged people to contemplate the interaction between cosmic forces and nature, and this gave rise to a central part of the Emperor's contribu-tion to society, the calendar.

This was produced each year so the people would know when to sow and harvest their crops and expect seasonal changes. This was 'the harmony of the elements' and part of the reckoning included observations of the phases of the moon, the appearance of stars and predictions of eclipses and comets. Astronomy became vital and from the eleventh century a separate department existed to assist the Emperor. There was a steady need for more accurate information, as failure to predict an event indicated that the heavens were not favouring that particular Emperor; constant experimentation led to the invention of the world's first clock in about 1084. The massive instrument was secreted in the Emperor's palace, where later, not knowing what it was, the Mongols destroyed it without its existence ever becoming public knowledge.

The Mings were ousted in 1644 as a result of the Emperor Wanli interfering in a dispute along his border between two Manchus. It turned out that Wanli supported the losing side and the victorious Manchu chief invaded northern China. By 1630 the Manchu campaign was well under way, and that year civil war also broke out. A rebel

general marched on Peking, whereupon the Emperor committed sui-
cide. The loyal Ming army called upon the Manchus to adopt their
cause and this gave them the opportunity to seize the throne. The
first Manchu Emperor, Sunchih spent his entire reign subjugating
the Mings, and his successor, Kangxi, carried on the campaign and
completed the conquest by 1683. He wisely retained the Chinese
administrators and proceeded to embrace all things Chinese.

Before the Manchus seized power, the first European merchants
had appeared. As expected, the Portuguese caused considerable
trouble and, even worse, refused to go away. Eventually they were
allowed to remain in Macau, a remote part of the Celestial Empire,
on condition that they did not allow any other barbarians to pass
up the estuary to Canton. This was in response to the arrival of
a new species who did even more damage: these 'red-haired barbarians'*, the Dutch, were very aggressive and refused to be taken
in by the hollow promises of Chinese officials, whose major concern
was that the Son of Heaven be not bothered by disturbances which
might result in an investigation, exposing their own corruption.

When the mandarins (an Indian term for a government official
adopted by the Portuguese for use all over the Far East) refused
to give the Dutch a cargo, their fleet sailed into the Canton estuary
and Willem Bontekoe, one of the captains, in his book entitled *Memorable Description of the East India Voyage 1618–25* recalled how it was
'to see if, through fear of our enmity, we could move them to traffic
[trade] with us'. When this was ineffective, the Dutch plundered
and burnt down several villages, and then 'went to and fro bringing
together all the Chinese we could take'. These prisoners were herded
on to the ships and 'we brought them all to the Pescadores ... as
much [many] as 1,400 in number, who were afterwards taken to
Batavia and sold'.

The red-haired barbarians were eventually allowed to settle on the
island of Formosa, which was then outside Manchu jurisdiction, so
long as they abandoned the Pescadores. Having witnessed the Dutch
acts of violence and piracy, it was little wonder that the arrival of
the first English ships under John Weddell in 1637 was viewed with
hostility and alarm.

Weddell began by attempting to trade with the Portuguese at Macau,
but found the settlement devoid of goods and unwilling to offer any
help lest their actions caused a confrontation with the Chinese, so

* To the Chinese red hair could be any shade from blond to dark brown.

he decided to sail straight up the Pearl River towards Canton. He anchored in the Bocca Tigris channel under a disused fort and spent the next two months either being fobbed off by the Chinese or being the victim of 'Noretti', a Chinese con-man who masqueraded as an interpreter. A letter was received from Canton telling the English to leave and he read this out as an invitation to open trade. Noretti took Weddell's factors and money up to Canton, whereupon they were arrested. Weddell then went on a rampage, destroying the fort, burning a village and sinking several junks before returning to Macau, where the Jesuits helped to secure the release of the factors and some money. As far as the Chinese were concerned, the Englishman's visit had proved that all red-haired barbarians were extremely dangerous and to be prohibited from entering China.

One group of Europeans who were welcomed when they first appeared in Peking in 1601 were the Jesuit scholar-missionaries. At first their deputation was treated with suspicion and they were thrown into prison, but, on release, their knowledge caused several high-ranking officials to treat them well. The Emperor Wanli was very pleased with his presents and was especially taken with a chiming clock, the first timepiece seen in China for over 500 years. When it broke, the leader of the missionaries, Matteo Ricci, was called to the palace and met the Emperor, who gave him a position on the very prestigious Board of Astronomy, the body responsible for supplying the calculations used in compiling the Imperial calendar. The Jesuits survived the revolution which brought the Manchus to power and contrived to achieve their continued presence in Peking with a clever policy of only sending missionaries who were well schooled in the sciences and therefore useful to the Emperor. Religious discussion was carefully avoided by both sides and, apart from one short expulsion lasting from 1616 to 1623, the missionaries prospered. The Chinese were amazed by the high standard of European learning, but could not review their conception of Peking being at the centre of the world and so, when a chart drawn by Mercator was given them, it had to be altered to show China in a more central position.

In 1656 the Dutch sent an embassy to China, which was received and treated in the same way as those from China's near neighbours, and, when the Europeans tried to start negotiating with the Emperor after their presentation, the officials were horrified. It had been difficult enough for the Chinese to accept that the Dutch were any more than seaborne pirates, but the Emperor was gracious and sent the standard letter with an addendum permitting them to send one ship every eight years.

The embassy may have been a disaster but, when a report was published in Holland, it was avidly read by all of Europe's East India Companies and did increase the stock of knowledge on China. What the Dutch did not grasp, however, was that all embassies to the Emperor were purely ceremonial; they put their lack of success down to plotting by the Portuguese Jesuits because they were Protestants in just the same way as Weddell had wrongly attributed his failure to other Europeans' intrigues with the Chinese. Catholic France did take up the challenge though and, after a Belgian, Ferdinand Verbiest, was made head of the mission and President of the Board of Astronomy in 1676, began to send Frenchmen to China as missionaries.

Verbiest was as close as any European had ever been to an Emperor of China, at this time a broad minded man named Kangxi, and he undoubtedly played a large part in persuading him to issue an Imperial edict in 1685 which opened China's ports to foreign ships.

The Jesuits continued to be influential throughout Kangxi's reign, which ended in 1722, but, soon after his death, a dispute arose between them and the Dominicans over which Chinese word from several choices best represented their conception of the Christian God. The new Emperor, Yung Cheng, became involved and gave his decision that the word would be that favoured by the Jesuits. At this the Dominicans complained to the Pope, who overturned the Emperor's ruling, but when this news was conveyed to him, Yung Cheng was furious that a barbarian should presume to question the decision of the Son of Heaven, especially over a matter involving the Chinese language. In 1727 the teaching of the Christian faith was prohibited, and the only priests permitted to remain in China were those retained on the Board of Astronomy and other places where they were useful.

The English East India Company or, to give its correct title, The Governor and Company of Merchants of London Trading to the East Indies, had been formed by Royal Charter of Queen Elizabeth i on 31 December 1600. Its ships made their first voyage several months later to the Spice Islands, which now form Malaysia and Indonesia, and found the Portuguese and Dutch already well established. The English persisted and the first years were turbulent ones with huge profits being seen as often as large losses, but factories or trading bases were built in a number of places, often adjacent to those of their competitors.

By the 1620s the Dutch had virtually expelled the Portuguese and were almost at war with the English East India Company. Conditions became so bad that the directors in London decided to close many of the Spice Island factories and concentrate on trading with India and other Far East countries. Expeditions were sent to Japan, Indo-China (then known as Cochin China), Thailand and Burma, and several factories were precariously established. These were set up mainly to try and deal with Chinese merchants, as silk was a valuable commodity in England, and by the 1630s the Court of Directors (known as the Court) was looking to China herself.

The first Company ship to arrive in Macau was the *Hinde* in 1644. She found the settlement 'destitute of all sorts of commodities' and complained bitterly about the large sum (3,500 pieces of eight) demanded by the Chinese for measuring the ship. It was known from the reports of Weddell's ships that duty was levied on the basis of the size of the vessel, but, despite neverending requests to be told the formula used in the calculation, no one ever learned how the Chinese arrived at the sum they demanded and it was generally believed to be a purely arbitrary figure based on their estimation of how much the ship could afford. The *Hinde* stayed in Macau for several months and found the Portuguese friendly, but unable to supply the silks and sugar which they sought; she was only able to load a small cargo of chinaware and gold.

During the 1650s intelligence from the Portuguese in Goa and other factories in the Spice Islands told of a rebellion sweeping China, with trade and everything else consequently in disarray, thus the Company, in any case weakened by the English Civil War, did not send another ship until 1664. This, the *Surat*, found Macau extremely depressed and, as the Chinese had not permitted any ships to leave for over two years, nineteen vessels lay in the harbour in various states of decay. The Portuguese were also smarting from a heavy fine levied five years earlier when two private English ships (inter-lopers), *King Ferdinand* and *Richard and Martha*, had sailed off before paying measurage fees. Repayment was demanded, but refused on the grounds that 'those were none of the Company's ships and it concerned us not'. For a time the situation was rather delicate, but eventually the *Surat*'s cargo of indigo and pepper was landed and some sold, but, after deducting the Chinese fees, no profit was made.

This disappointment prompted the Court to try for indirect trade and so ships were sent to Taiwan in 1671 and to Hanoi the next year. In Hanoi they found silk in reasonable quantity and a small factory was established which, faced with a grasping king who con-trolled all prices, eked out a miserable existence until 1697. Taiwan appeared more promising as its ruler, Koxinga, was one of the last independent Mings and still at war with the Manchus. His territory also included the mainland port of Amoy and, in succeeding years, a fair amount of trading was done, mainly in exchange for guns and ammunition.

The Company's directors were unshakable in their belief that Canton was potentially the best port in China and every ship in the region carried instructions to call in at Macau if practicable. In 1673 the *Return* was sent to Nagasaki in Japan, but found everything there too expensive so her captain 'resolved to make for the port of Macau where it was hoped the Portuguese would allow [us] to stay and perhaps trade'. She was well received there and told that trade was possible, but only for cash and so, 'As there was no cash, only merchandise, little was done but the chief merchant, Mr Delboe, felt it established a precedent for future negotiation.' The ship departed full of optimism and years later, when the Company's historian wrote of the trade with China, he considered that 'this may be the incident from which the Chinese trade with the East India Company can be traced'.

In the following two years the *Carolina* and *Loyal Adventure* arrived in Macau and did good trade with Chinese merchants who had, somewhat clandestinely, established themselves on a nearby island known as Lampaco. Trade continued in Taiwan, but it was subject to the changing fortunes of Koxinga and the factory closed in 1681 after he suffered a military setback. In Macau the *Carolina*'s merchants, now rechristened supracargoes, were told by the officials that the Emperor was 'much enraged against the English and Hollanders ... [as] they do yearly assist the King of Taiwan with ammunition and powder to fight against him'. She was ordered out but managed to do $19,000* worth of business at Lampaco before seven men-of-war junks appeared and forced her to sail.

Whilst the *Carolina* was in Chinese waters, the directors in London had found the craze for tea was gaining momentum and sent out four more ships, each with orders to bring back $1,000 worth. These vessels found conditions difficult, but the directors persisted and sent one or two ships each year for the remainder of the decade. Most spent many months in Amoy or, after 'a padre who lives with the Emperor' told the supracargoes that Nanking had much fine silk, tried that port. The delays experienced were mainly caused by the ponderous methods of the Chinese officials and were frustrating for

---

* In the Far East the Spanish eight real (piece of eight) or dollar was the standard currency. This was converted at four to the pound sterling.

all, including the sailors who, plied with strong, cheap drink by unscrupulous Chinese, sometimes ran amok. A couple of incidents, – the shooting of a thief in 1684 and a fracas in the customs house when a drunken sailor broke in during 1688 – caused much trouble.

When the 730-ton *Defence* appeared at Macau in 1689, she was the largest English ship to date to be sent to China and, because such a large vessel was obviously full of silver, was immediately promised a 'chop'* to begin trading. This was an excellent start for her chief supracargo, Mr Yale, but the remainder of his stay was full of problems, which began when the *Defence*'s commander, Captain Heath, refused to take the ship into the Pearl River. He was eventually persuaded to do so, but was angered when the Chinese insisted on taking away a mast to prevent the ship from leaving. They then refused to measure the ship, probably until they could gauge how much money was available, so the supracargoes went up to Canton and negotiated contracts for sugar and tutenague (spelter). The Chinese then announced a measurage fee of 2,484 taels, which Mr Yale knew to be excessive and hotly contested it until the figure was reduced to 1,500 taels to the customs and 300 to the *hoppo*.†

Captain Heath, in the meantime, was becoming increasingly upset over the restrictions imposed on his ship and crew. About four months after their arrival, he took and armed party ashore to retrieve the mast. There was a major fracas when he landed and eventually one Chinaman was killed and the sailors, plus mast, were forced to retire rapidly, leaving ten of their number, including the ship's doctor who was seriously wounded, behind. Mr Yale offered 2,000 taels towards the Chinese demand for 5,000 taels compensation, but there was to be no negotiation and the ship had no alternative but to sail, leaving their companions behind to be looked after by the Portuguese and a friendly Chinese merchant.

There were no successes in the 1690s and problems with the formation of a rival company in England caused most ships to sail to ports where their cargoes would be guaranteed, but, in August 1699, the *Macclesfield* anchored near Macau. In only a few days, rather than the customary weeks, Portuguese and Chinese officials came on board and welcomed them with promises of trade. A supracargo who had been to Canton before recognized a merchant who fortunately spoke

---

* Literally, an officially sealed document, but in practice anything from a permit for travel to an order from a Chinese official.
† The *Hoppo* was usually a Manchu and would not normally be personally involved in such a small matter. The English described any customs officer as *hoppo*.

Portuguese (which was a condition of a supracargo's employment) and so direct negotiation without an interpreter resulted in his offering to purchase their entire cargo. About a month later the *hoppo* came in person to the ship, signalling a change in policy which was probably the result of the fact that news of the Emperor's 1685 decree opening ports to foreigners had at last filtered through to Canton. The ship was measured and the *hoppo*, 'in order to prove his desire to favour us', reduced the amount due from 1,200 taels to 480. The supracargoes seized the opportunity to ask for chops giving free trade and unlimited access to Canton, which to their delight, arrived soon afterwards. Unfortunately the chops limited trade to Macau and required the English, not the Chinese merchants, to pay export duties on the goods; these 'mistakes' were corrected when pointed out, but future supracargoes became only too familiar with similar 'errors' and were forced to be constantly vigilant.

On 7 October the *Macclesfield* was invited to move up to Whampoa and Mr Douglas, the Chief supracargo, had good reason to be satisfied, as he had already achieved more than any previous voyage. He then went on to Canton and began to negotiate for purchases, but soon discovered that all the merchants were quoting exactly the same prices and were obviously working together. Among these merchants were ones described as 'privileged', who operated under the auspices of high-ranking officials including the *Chun-quin* (a Manchu general), *Chuntuck* (viceroy or high commissioner) and *Fuyuen* (provincial governor), but the supracargoes made a contract with an independent named Hunshunquin.

For the next nine months Mr Douglas had to fight for everything he achieved and was beset with problems. The first occurred when seven members of the ship's crew went ashore to pitch a tent and were viciously attacked by upwards of eighty French sailors commanded by the captain of their ship. After an official apology was demanded and received, the supracargoes returned to Canton only to find that their merchant had been imprisoned, apparently at the instigation of the 'great mandarin's merchants', who wanted part of the business. No sooner was this problem overcome than the Chinese levied a hitherto unmentioned duty on woollen goods; then Hunshunquin declared that much of their cloth was inferior or damaged and demanded discounts. Arguing over this point continued until early December and, within days of agreement being reached over prices of sales and purchases, a Spanish galleon arrived at Macau from Manila with $500,000 on board, dramatically increasing the price of silk. More negotiating followed as Hunshunquin tried to pull out of the deal and the ship lost the monsoon. Chinese officials became involved and ordered the *Macclesfield* to leave, but Douglas refused to go until his affairs were settled and so the *hoppo* suggested he take over the contract for the woollens and offered 6,500 taels against an original price of 22,000 taels. The merchants then delivered 12,000 taels worth of second quality silk and the dispute escalated. Hapless interpreters who gave the wrong answers found themselves in chains, but finally a deal was struck and the ship sailed on 18 July 1700. She carried a cargo of silk, tea, pepper, fans (100,000), porcelain, musk, inlaid tables and gold, by far the most successful and comprehensive cargo of any ship to trade in China to date. The *Macclesfield* made her way up to Chusan and bought a further quantity of silk before heading back for England, which she reached on 1 July 1701.

After this success, China was comparatively deluged with English ships, an average of six each year arriving between 1701 and 1704. They divided almost equally between the three ports of Canton, Amoy and Chusan, and most managed to come away with a good cargo after varying degrees of difficulty. In England, Parliament, under pressure from the weavers, passed an Act forbidding the wearing of imported silk cloth, so the Company ordered that only raw silk be purchased. The Chinese did not want to sell it in this form and tried to promote tea and porcelain instead, but these were still in limited demand and there was always a battle for the 'right' cargo. The Company also experienced problems with export cargoes as its charter stipulated that at least ten per cent of the value of a ship's stock be comprised of woollens, which were of virtually no interest to the Chinese, whose preoccupation was silver, although lead was considered 'as good as money'. Strangely, gold had never formed part of the Chinese currency and, as this could be bought cheaply, it normally made up the difference between the value of the imports (cash and cloth) and goods purchased, as only rarely did a ship come away with all the cargo she wanted. Back in England a profit of nearly fifty per cent could be made on gold by selling to the Royal Mint.

From time to time more problems appeared. One year a merchant who had previously dealt only in salt went to Peking and paid the Emperor's son 42,000 taels for a chop which gave him exclusive rights to trade with the English. The fact that he had no goods to sell did not seem to matter in the granting of the permit and the arrangement was just a clever ploy to get paid off by the proper merchants, but it did hold up a number of ships.

On another occasion the *hoppo* retired, but stayed on for a year whilst his replacement learned all the tricks of the job, so there were two *hoppos*, both of whom had to be appeased with bribes and duties. Then, in 1704, a figure of four per cent duty appeared on a document as an extra charge. After investigation, it emerged that in previous years the linguist appointed to each ship had to pay the *hoppo* one per cent of the value of its bill of lading as a bribe for being given the job and likewise the merchants paid him three per cent. Now the *hoppo* decided that this sum would come from supracargoes and no one ever found out if the merchants and translators continued to pay it as well.

Another method of extortion favoured by the junior customs officers was to hold up all the bales of silk, when the ship was in a hurry to leave, on the pretext of opening each one to see if any of the cloth was yellow, a colour forbidden to export. A 'present' always sorted this out and the Chinese were quite blatant in naming the sum they sought, which at least made things easier, though no less odious.

As trade became more regular, sugar was only rarely exported and even silk declined in importance as tea drinking reached national proportions in England and her colonies. The Court sent out the *Kent* in 1704 with instructions to bring back 117 tons of tea and only 22 tons of raw silk, but, as previous supracargoes had experienced difficulty in filling much smaller orders, this ship and others like her had to buy other goods to complete the lading. The Canton merchants were simply not used to carrying such large stocks and so supracargoes were instructed to tell them that they would purchase tea in any quantity, but the Court also warned 'by no means contract with them beforehand for what is bought, lest they should oblige you take it although it may be never so bad'.

All three ports were regularly used up to 1715, when Amoy was abandoned as a result of an interloper ship whose commander, when he felt cheated, captured a junk and took it to Madras.

By this time the Company's supracargoes had established a regular working relationship with the *hoppo* and, as soon as the new season's ships arrived off Macau, the supracargoes' first task was to make sure no new prohibitions or difficulties had been introduced. Everything being in order, the ship sailed up the river to the Bocca Tigris, where the *hoppo*'s people would come on board. At this point the supracargoes put forward their request for conditions of trade. These normally consisted of: unrestricted access to the *hoppo* and all merchants, protection from insults (which were a regular irritation in

Canton, accusations of horrible crimes committed by Europeans being fixed up in public places, taunts and jeers in the streets and even physical attack), free choice of linguists and other Chinese servants, free passage without being searched to and from the ship for the supracargoes and captain, provision of all stores and materials for repairs to the ship, no duty for goods on board or landed which were not for sale, and, most importantly, to be told all duties and other demands when the ship was measured and at no other time. From 1715, the *hoppo* generally agreed to all these with the exception of the last, which always infuriated the supracargoes as they never knew whether, just before the ship was ready to depart, some new charge would be mentioned, a trick which the Chinese, knowing the ship could not leave before all payments were received, often tried.

When the chop for trade was issued, the ship would proceed up to Whampoa. After the long voyage goods needed drying out and many repairs were necessary, so the ship was stripped of all its sails and spars, water casks, ballast and rigging, which were taken ashore and kept in a large tent known as a bankshall. About a month after arriving the ship was measured and by December there could be twenty ships of all nationalities at anchor. The sailors remained either on board or at their bankshall for the entire six months the ship was in port, and one day each week the Chinese for a fee permitted exercise on one of two nearby islands. This was carefully controlled so that each nationality was on shore *en masse* on a different day because, even though Whampoa was a strictly neutral port, in time of war fights between sailors occasionally broke out.

The supracargoes and captains remained for most of the time in Canton, where they hired the same factory year after year. After 1715 supracargoes of different ships were instructed by the Court to co-operate with each other as prices had been pushed up when each ship individually tried to complete their lading in the shortest time. Later all the supracargoes were given a position in a 'council' and the ships were considered as one entity, goods being first bought in quantity and then distributed between them. The cargo to be carried depended on whether the ship was to sail straight for England or stop for further trading in India. If it was England, a cargo of tea, chinaware and silk was purchased in quantities according to stocks and what the supracargoes were told by the Court was most in demand. A ship going to India would carry a much more varied cargo including copper, sugar, quicksilver (mercury), camphor wood, tutenague and alum (salt). Every ship received a standard letter forbidding her officers from purchasing musk 'lest the scent spoil your tea'.

Most goods were purchased by the Chinese *'picul'* (133⅓ lbs), although a chest of tea weighed 250 lbs because the supracargoes bought the leaves loose and made their own containers. Chinaware is noted as being packed in tubs, bundles, half and full chests and was cushioned with sago to help protect it against breakage. When all the goods were ready, usually in November and December, they were sent down to Whampoa in Chinese river boats to be loaded aboard. The ships were completely empty at this stage and so the ballast bars (kintledge) were put on board first, followed by cases of chinaware, which acted as extra ballast and then the tea and silks. Once the ship was ready, the 'grand chop', permitting departure, was requested and, if all went well, they sailed between mid-December and mid-January, arriving home about six months later.

1720 brought two new problems. The first came about when a group of dissatisfied English ship owners persuaded the Emperor of Austria to form an East India company which was actually nothing more than a front for their operations. The English East India Company responded angrily and instructed its ships to sail with all speed to Canton to arrive 'before the Ostenders' and to buy all the tea which was available, as 'cost what it will, we must try to make these interlopers sick of their voyages for tea'. As it turned out the 'Ostenders' arrived first, but at the end of the year something much more serious occupied the supracargoes' attention: the merchants of Canton formed themselves into a 'guild' and fixed all prices.

Four ships were sent out the following year and soon learned of the new system. At the same time the supracargoes discovered that a high commissioner from Peking was in Canton and the *hoppo* was very keen to show the ships being measured and allow him the pick of the European 'curiosities' (mainly clocks) which the captains had been in the habit of bringing to sell to officials as status symbols. The supracargoes refused to bring the ships up to Whampoa and told the *chuntuck*'s agent that they would not be able to trade unless the 'society' of merchants was dissolved. This would have been a serious embarrassment for the *hoppo*, so the *chuntuck* called the merchants together and instructed them to 'burn the instrument which they had entered into for forming the society', after which business proceeded as usual.

The next year the ships discovered that the posts of governor (*fuyuen*) and *hoppo* were held by one man who demanded payments for both offices. Later two instances of trouble with sailors were only solved with large bribes. In 1727 only one ship was sent out and her supracargo, in an effort to reduce drunkenness, included a request for no *samshoo* (spirit) houses to be built at Whampoa when he submitted the usual list of conditions to the *hoppo*. He wrote in his journal the amount paid for the ship's measurage and added an additional sum of 1,950 taels bribe. The system of bribery was a major feature of Chinese trade and corruption among officials was absolutely endemic, but this is the first mention of a proscribed sum being levied before trading even began and it was to be a point of contention for many years.

When this lone ship returned home with a good cargo, London again sent four ships in 1728. These were greeted with the news that the four per cent duty first imposed in 1704 had been increased to ten per cent. The ensuing dispute escalated to the extent that supracargoes from all the European companies marched in a body to the city gates, brushed past the guard and presented themselves at the *chuntuck*'s palace. He eventually saw them, but refused to reduce the tax saying 'they might go if they pleased, other ships would come'. The ships did leave without proper cargoes and the resulting drop in income for the officials obviously had some effect, for next year it was noted, 'We are not informed categorically of the result of the dispute over the ten per cent, but there is every reason to believe that the merchants paid it.' In 1736 the duty was abolished by the new Emperor, who insisted instead that all guns and arms be deposited with the officials, leaving the ship completely defenceless. The supracargoes categorically refused and made 'considerable presents to the *Tsontock*' (another term for the viceroy which was generally used in place of *chuntuck* after about 1725). Next year it was noted, 'We have heard nothing about the guns.'

In 1742 something truly extraordinary happened at the mouth of the Pearl River which was to cause hitherto unimagined problems for the supracargoes and Chinese merchants alike: the man-of-war HMS *Centurion* appeared and her commander, Commodore George Anson, asked for assistance with repairs and complete reprovisioning. This, the first warship to appear on the Chinese coast, was nearly three times as big as an ordinary merchant ship and bristled with sixty guns; she was a positive monster so far as the Chinese were concerned and was to be treated with the utmost suspicion. As the sea was only inhabited by merchants, with whom they were acquainted, and pirates, a ship which refused to be measured on the grounds that it had no goods on board must fall into the latter category. The Portuguese and the English both knew that this would be the Chinese attitude and neither were keen to be seen to give any assistance to the *Centurion* for fear of reprisals, but at the same time they did not want Anson to come to them, so it was a serious dilemma. For the Chinese, whilst this terrifying vessel remained at the Taipa anchorage near Macau, she could be watched and so the Macau *hoppo* was dispatched to look over the ship. He was received by Commodore Anson, who desired a chop to go up to Canton the next day. This was, of course, out of the question and the *hoppo* said as much, only to be told that, if it was not forthcoming, an armed party would proceed upriver anyway. The chop arrived next day.

If Anson was not already fully aware of the problems he was causing his countrymen, they wasted no time in telling him as soon as he appeared at Whampoa. The *hongists,* through whom the only access could be gained to senior officials, were unable to help as any approach would be seen as that particular merchant supporting the ship and to do such a thing would certainly lead to banishment from Canton at the least and possibly even execution. The supracargoes decided the best course was to supply Anson's needs from their own stocks and, during December and January, over 2,000 lbs of bread and nearly as much pork were smuggled aboard. The Chinese conveniently turned a blind eye to this as they were desperate for the huge pirate to leave before news of his presence reached Peking.

Anson returned to Taipa and entertained the *hoppo* and several other officials to dinner on board. They stayed for five hours, were mystified by the knives and forks provided for their meal, drank a large quantity of wine (without any apparent effect) and were told that all Anson wanted to do was leave as soon as his ship was repaired. This was exactly what they hoped to hear and, no doubt after some rapidly passed messages to Canton, within days the ship was swarming with Chinese workmen. By early March 1743 the repairs were complete and, to everybody's delight, the *Centurion* sailed away.

Then, on 11 July, the worst possible happened: the *Centurion* reappeared together with another ship in tow which she had obviously captured. As part of the war with Spain, Anson had sailed directly towards the Philippines, where he captured the annual Manila galleon on her way to Lisbon with over £800,000 worth of silver and gold on board, and now wanted still more provisions for the voyage home to England. He decided to avoid the Macau *hoppo*, who was seen to be just a minion of those in Canton, and sailed straight into the Bocca Tigris channel, anchoring beneath the same deserted fort as Weddell had chosen over a century before. The officials arrived to measure the ships and were politely told this would not be permitted. They returned to Canton and soon afterwards the Viceroy heard that there was a large amount of silver, which was very interesting, and that all the prisoners on board were being treated well, which did not make sense. The Chinese immediately executed any prisoner they took and considered it perfectly honourable, so the fact that these were still alive only added to the mystery which now enveloped the pirate ship. The Viceroy sent an official to demand the release of the prisoners, which Anson (although keen to be rid of them) refused, hoping to use them as a bargaining point, and this made him look a terrible demon, suspected of proposing to perform some unimaginable vileness at a later date.

Anson prevailed on the supracargoes to stop trading until his request for re-provisioning was met by the Chinese, but hardly any supplies were coming aboard and the *hoppo* was still talking about paying dues, so there was nothing for it but to go directly to the Viceroy. With forty sailors in full dress uniforms, Anson went to the Company's factory in Canton to await an invitation, but failed to understand that there was no possibility whatsoever of the Viceroy being seen to bend to the will of a pirate as it would be a loss of face. After waiting for two months Anson sent a letter demanding to see the Viceroy, but as luck would have it, the next day a fire broke out in Canton which destroyed over 100 shops and several streets of warehouses before the sailors were mobilized into demolishing a street of houses, which acted as a fire break and contained the blaze.

This provided the Viceroy with the perfect excuse for seeing the intruder without any loss of face at all and the following day Anson received an invitation to an audience. All the Company's supracargoes and captains took the opportunity to attend this unique event and Anson was briefed to mention their various complaints. On the appointed day, 10,000 Chinese troops with banners and flags assembled outside the palace and Anson was carried in a covered chair amid much pomp and ceremony. The Viceroy sat on his throne and, in a rare concession, provided a chair for the Commodore whilst all the others stood. Anson was thanked for his assistance in extinguishing the fire and asked his desire, which was to receive provisions and leave. The Viceroy immediately instructed a writer to prepare the necessary chop and then listened in astonished silence as Anson had the effrontery to suggest he might care to relax some of the restrictions on the merchants. After a long pause one of the Company's linguists said 'that he did not believe an answer would be given' and the audience came to an end, the Viceroy regaining his composure and politely wishing Anson a 'prosperous journey back to Europe'.

The *Centurion* was soon filled with everything she needed, the Spanish prize was sold to the citizens of Macau, who also agreed to look after the prisoners and, in mid-December, followed by a host of Chinese junks, the great ship set off down the river. The fort where they had first anchored was manned this time by an impressive group of figures who were wearing what appeared to be splendid silver breast plates. On examination through a telescope these were seen to be made of silver paper. The Chinese were certainly an un-fathomable people and her strength or weakness was something no one could quite determine.

The outcome of this display of power by the English nation was not what the supracargoes had hoped for and the matter was con-veniently forgotten as an unpleasant experience. What did happen was that the Chinese were reinforced in their perception of England as a country populated by pirates on a massive scale and therefore all Englishmen were completely untrustworthy and dangerous.

In the wake of Anson, although not because of him, the Company continued to expand the Canton market, sending never less than eight ships each year between 1747 and 1751, even though the supra-cargoes continued to find conditions oppressive and had much to complain about. The main point of contention at this time was the system of 'security' which had been introduced in the 1730s and required one merchant to be responsible for the payment of customs duty for both goods imported and exported on each ship. This meant that, if the merchant in question did not purchase and sell all the goods appertaining to the vessel for which he was security (which was virtually unheard of), he had to pay the total duty to the *hoppo* and then collect that which was owed by the other merchants, often a difficult task. The security for each ship was also responsible for showing the *hoppo* the European 'curiosities' and, as he normally paid about a quarter of the true price, it was an expensive proposition and the supracargoes, who could not trade unless they had a security, often had difficulty in persuading a merchant to stand for a ship.

The Court in London was told in 1736 about the attitude of the Chinese officials towards 'the merchants of their own country, who they place in a very low and contemptible rank', but it obviously never occurred to the supracargoes that they might be considered in the same light because, in 1753, in a report about negotiations with the *hoppo* over the security controversy they wrote: 'His pride and ignorance [is] so extraordinary that he did not vouchsafe to return common civilities to any of us [even] though we paid him the highest respect.' The debate continued interminably and in 1755 the number of merchants who were available to take on the responsibility was reduced even further when an edict was issued limiting the number of *hongists* who could trade with Europeans. Finally, it was decided that the *hoppo* would simply nominate a *hongist* to be security for each ship, so the supracargoes at least did not have to persuade them with promises of extra business.

On several occasions the Company decided to try trading at Amoy or Limpo (the actual town of Ningpo was a short distance from this anchorage), but the advantage of these ports not charging the same duty as Canton was offset by the lack of goods and inability of merchants to guarantee delivery. In 1756, the *Griffin* traded at Limpo/ Ningpo and when, the following year, the *Onslow* arrived there, she was told to proceed to Chusan, where the supracargoes learned that the *tsontock* of Canton had persuaded the Emperor to restrict all future European trade to his city. The *Onslow* had to pay quadruple duty and double measurage for her meagre cargo, and at her departure the *towya*, the senior Chinese official, told them 'it would be folly to come back next year', so she became the last ship to trade there.

The supracargoes who went down to Macau from Canton in May 1760 did not have long to wait for the first ship of the new season as the *Valentine* arrived on 2 June, followed soon after by the *Suffolk*. They described how Admiral Pocock had detained them in India the previous year to 'assist in possible battles against the French', and also gave the more interesting news that the *Denham*, *Oxford* and *Pocock* Indiamen would be following shortly. This was the first inkling they had of how many ships would be in Canton for 1760; it was considerably fewer than the thirteen which had arrived the year before. This lack of warning always made their lives difficult due to the necessity for ordering tea in advance, and all the supracargoes could do each year was to make estimates based on the previous year. They had contracted for enough tea to fill nine or ten ships and, if some did not sail directly from England, there would be a large surplus. In previous years this had not been so important as it could be stored at the factory, but if the yearly migration to Macau continued at the end of this season, the extra tea would pose a serious problem.

On 5 June the supracargoes ordered a boat for Canton and were dismayed to learn that part of the new regulations demanded that they have a chop for this journey. One of the *hongists* agreed to request it and suggested it might take five or six days. They wrote a letter for any ship heading to Limpo telling it to come instead to Whampoa and waited for the permit, which eventually took three weeks.

The journey from Macau to Canton took a whole day, but at least the heat and humidity of the mid-summer was less oppressive on the river. In Canton it became so hot during July and August that 'scarce anyone stirs in the middle of the day ... and even in the night it is so hot as not a little to interrupt sleep'. At Whampoa the sailors found themselves plagued by swarms of insects which the Chinese called 'horse mosquitoes'. Their sting was painful and, as Surgeon John McQueen of the *Britannia* discovered in 1758, 'excite intolerable heat and itching that you can't forbear scratching although it makes it ten times worse'. Everyone slept under nets of 'green silk'.

Leaving Macau, the boat passed numerous barren islands in the mouth of the river estuary, which is called the Bogue and is more like an inland sea, so wide that on a hazy day both banks cannot be seen at once. Along the shore, which was mainly flat, were many small bays, each with a settlement and rice plantation. These were notorious pirate haunts and were avoided by all except the occasional country ship which brought a cargo of contraband opium, although in 1760 this trade was still in its infancy and the Company had issued strong directives to ensure none of its vessels carried the drug. About six hours' sail brought the ship to the Bocca Tigris, a narrow twenty-mile channel leading to Whampoa enclosed by high ground on which the Chinese had built several forts, now deserted. The river was shallower here and, although small boats were not affected, many heavily laden Indiamen had run aground on one particular sand bank called the Second Bar and had to time their departure to coincide with high tide.

The land each side is quite hilly as the river nears Whampoa and, for the European, the sight is quite extraordinary as every inch of ground is cultivated with rice, wheat, vegetables and fruit trees. Even the steepest hills are terraced and the lush green spectacle is a complete contrast from the barren islands near Macau. At the first of the larger islands, Danes, the river forks into a little used waterway called Blenheim Passage and, to the right, the main anchorage near Whampoa Island is in a channel between it and Danes Island, where the sailors took their exercise. Whampoa was where the ships built their bankshalls, and the small town became a hive of activity as the season began with new shops under construction and old buildings, eaten away by termites which infest the island, being dismantled.

The river craft continued towards Canton, keeping Whampoa island on its left, and the view to the right is of wide fertile valleys together with the occasional pagoda, and several streams run into the main river. As Canton approached the number of boats multiplied until, in front of the walled city, there were tens of thousands including a complete floating town.

When John McQueen went to Canton he described the houses as being 'in general low and built with white stone, the windows are almost all of oyster shells. Tradesmen's shops of all sorts almost are very numerous and some of them are very grand and rich.' These were probably the ones nearest the row of European factories just west of the city walls on the waterfront. These buildings were very deep from front to back, almost 350 feet, but with quite a narrow facade. The English was the widest of all at 120 feet and also had the most impressive entrance with a two-level portico known as the verandah, which was supported by Roman columns, five deep and four across. Unlike the others, the English factory had direct access on to the river via a set of stone steps cut into the embankment. Between these and the building, only a matter of a few feet, was a tall flagpole flying the Union Jack. The other factories also flew their own flags and were set slightly back from the river, separated from it by an open square called Respondentia Walk, where the Europeans took their exercise.

Inside the English factory the ground floor contained approximately seven large rooms where the business of storing, grading and packing the tea and chinaware was done. The first floor was given over entirely to living accommodation, and a fine dining-room at the front gave directly on to the balcony, which was extensively used on hot evenings. The cellar served as a strong-room for the large amounts of silver the ships carried, and the annual rent for the factory was a comparative bargain at 600 taels (£200).

Unfortunately, the *co-hong*, which had been formed earlier in the year, had not been disbanded and the supracargoes decided that they would delay unloading the ships in the hope that the *hoppo* would step in. The *Griffin* arrived two days after the factory was opened and she was told to do nothing other than unload empty water casks until the dispute was settled. The *hoppo* became curious as to why the normal volume of taxable merchandise was not coming through his customs houses and was told that the ships would not begin to unload until the *hongists* agreed to come forward individually to discuss the price they would offer for the cargoes and, after waiting nearly a month, he demanded that trading commence immediately.

During this time the English had approached their Dutch and Swedish counterparts in an attempt to form a united front to try to force the *hongists* to disband their association, and the Dutch were warned by the *tsontock*, 'You must not be led away by the false stories of the English.' On 21 August, after the *hoppo*'s ultimatum, there were five English ships at Whampoa and, if business did not begin, they would miss the monsoon, so a petition was sent to the *tsontock* asking him to allow them free trade.

Three days later came the reply:

Although the merchants tell you they are formed into a company, it matters not to the Emperor whether they are or not. If the merchants offer a low price for your goods, or demand high prices for theirs, upon being acquainted with it, we will give you all possible redress, and, if you can't get a tolerable profit upon your goods, you must not in future bring any as it is of very small consequence to this country. For the ships which are arrived you may do your business with any of the Emperor's merchants you please, and we have particularly ordered them to comply punctually with their contracts in order that the Europeans may return to their own country in proper time, and if you behave quietly and properly, you shall always meet with our favour and protection ... You must therefore proceed to do your business in the manner we have prescribed.

With this there was no alternative but to start unloading the ships and the order was duly given on 25 August. The supracargoes went down to Whampoa and met the 'Grand Mandarin', who measured the ships and this signified that the season had begun. During September, the goods were brought up to the factory, where they were checked by the *hongists* before distribution, and in October and November the tea began to arrive. The supracargoes had purchased three grades and insisted that the cheapest, Bohea, came first as it was to be loaded immediately on top of the chinaware. In April, before going down to Macau, they had ordered 29,650 piculs of tea or just under 4 million lbs altogether. The Bohea was packed into 360-lb chests; the next best tea, Singlo, went into 84-lb 'half chests'; and the top quality, Twankay, went into 67-lb boxes. By mid-October the roomy ground floor of the factory was full of empty chests and the tea was being delivered daily in sacks. Years before it had been purchased already in wooden chests, but some Twankays were found to have a layer of Bohea or even sawdust at the bottom, so the supracargoes paid a number of Chinese labourers to pack it whilst they watched. A supracargo not only had to be an excellent businessman, bargainer, diplomat and mathematician, but also a tea expert.

In November supracargo Francis Kinnersley fell ill and died on the 14th; he was buried in the European cemetery on French Island two days later. Fortunately three other supracargoes, who were due to oversee the business for the ships sailing straight from England, later arrived and they were able to help. Their vessels must have been delayed, for they did not appear during 1760 and everyone hoped that they had not been captured by the French. The *Denham*, one of the ships expected from India, was scuttled to avoid just this fate.

On 10 December, just as the last shipments were due to leave for Whampoa, Thomas Lockwood declared that he would be leaving with them. Francis Wood was hardly surprised: Lockwood had endured five seasons in Canton and must have been exhausted, especially since 1760 had been the most difficult year on record as far as dealing with the Chinese was concerned.

CHAPTER 3

≡

The Company's Marine Service

The first two voyages of the East India Company had been a great success, but by 1607 the ships, which had been purchased second hand in 1600, were either worn out or wrecked so the directors advertised for replacements, offering to buy at £30 per ton. The supply of large ships in England had always been limited and in the previous few years had been even further reduced by the energetic buying of the recently formed Dutch East India Company, thus the owners of the few large remaining vessels were not impressed with this sum and demanded up to £45 per ton. As this was considered outrageous, the Company decided the only alternative was to build its own vessels.

After taking a lease on docks on the Thames at Deptford in 1607, construction of the first purpose-built East India ships (the term East Indiaman was not coined until a later date) was soon underway. The first two, which cost £5 per ton, were the *Peppercorn* and the *Trades Increase*, which was the largest merchant ship built in England up to that time, rated at 1,296 tons. This was so impressive that the King was invited to launch her.

After much preparation, all was ready and on 30 December 1610 the Royal Family, together with a huge retinue, descended on Deptford. It seems that the *Trades Increase* was already in the river whilst the small pinnace, which the King named *Peppercorn*, was on a slipway. Apparently the pinnace stuck fast and would not go into the water, and the large ship would not move at all as the tide was lower than expected and she was touching bottom. Despite these mishaps a great banquet was held on board the *Trades Increase*, where they ate for the first time off Chinese porcelain. The Company's chairman, Sir Thomas Smyth, must have been in his element and was later 'to be graced with a great chain of gold, and a medal to be put about his neck by the King's own hands'.

The Deptford dock grew so quickly that by 1614 the Company was forced to search for another site. They finally settled on an area next to the already established Blackwall Yard, which was run by the Johnson family, who were cousins of the famous Petts, who were busy building great ships for the King. This dock had the added advantage of being lower down the river and could therefore easily handle the larger ships which the Company proposed building.

Blackwall was a low lying spot (properly known as the East Marsh), so called after a builder named Milend had constructed a flood bank along that stretch in 1377; the earth and clay he used were very dark, thus sailors coming up the Thames would see the 'black-wall'. It is located just to the east of a long bend known as the Isle of Dogs. People in a hurry would disembark there and climb some steps to the pathway and, by taking a horse into the City of London, would save themselves a considerable amount of time. The Company's new land adjoined these stairs.

By 1615 there were 21 ships adding up to a total of over 10,000 tons, and five years later this figure had increased to 40 major vessels with as many as 100 smaller ones. At this time the entire Port of London could only boast 10 ships of its own with a burden of over 200 tons, so the East India Company was making a major contribution to shipbuilding generally and, especially, towards the employment of mariners and craftsmen.

The Blackwall Yard was found to be a highly convenient site but, for some unexplained reason, the Company decided to use it primarily for repairing their ships, despite the prospering construction business going on next to them. As the land in this area was virtually undeveloped, the Company was able to purchase a considerable amount very cheaply and, after completing the dry dock, set to work on building a great collection of warehouses, offices, a slaughterhouse and odd stores, where they had a substantial workforce making almost everything a ship would need during a refit. This included a large store of timber (although most of the wood was sawn and cured at Reading in Berkshire) for making new masts, yards, spars and pulleys as well as replacing any weak planks on the hull and providing new sheathing to guard against woodworm, which was a major problem. There was also a sailmaker's store, where new canvas was sewn, and a spinning house for making the extra thick ropes which were peculiar to the East India Company and could not be supplied by the Muscovy Company, who imported most of England's rope from Russia. Perhaps the largest operation carried out at Blackwall was the iron foundry, where anchors, chains and a myriad other metal objects required by a ship were cast.

The Dethick family mansion at Blackwall was located between the

Company's chapel and the Company schoolhouse, and was so close to the yard that, during the mid-seventeenth century, Gilbert Dethick was forced to complain 'of the great annoyance to himself and the whole marsh at Blackwall from the blood and slubb issuing from the Company's slaughterhouse there, the stench being so noisome and offensive'.

At Deptford they also constructed a complex of buildings primarily used for victualling ships for the long voyage. In addition to the shipwrights' offices, there was a brewery for beer and cider, a bakery for biscuits and a place for salting the meat, which was originally purchased directly from the farmers, some of whom, conveniently, were directors of the Company. The directors were most concerned with the health of their sailors on a voyage, primarily, one suspects, out of the knowledge that ships had had to be abandoned in the past due to lack of fit crewmen, and they took great care to provide food of the highest possible quality, bombarding the butchers and bakers with precise instructions as to how to prepare things. One brewer was sent to prison for supplying beer that was considered bad.

Strangely, they were slow (as was the Royal Navy) to find a cure for scurvy, even though the commander of the first voyage, James Lancaster, had kept his ship free of the disease by supplying the men with lemon juice, but this is the only recorded use of this remedy for well over one hundred years. Some individual captains may have known the cure, but there seems to be no reason for concealing it and the only conclusion is that Lancaster's lemon juice was simply not recognized as having relieved scurvy. The Company's policy of ensuring good food seems well founded, for although the sailors complained about it, few died of food poisoning before reaching India or the Spice Islands.

Overseeing the huge infrastructure, which was incredibly highly developed for an organization so young, were three men each of whom had his own specialization and did not trespass on the others' ground. Once, when one did, he was dismissed by the Directors, who, according to the minutes of Court meetings, stated 'he had taken more upon him than belonged to his place'. These three most senior posts were: chief shipwright, whose duties were to build and repair the Company's ships; the clerk of the yard, who was in charge of the workforce and general running of the yards; and the ship's husband. This last officer was perhaps the most important as he was the only one to attend meetings of the Committee of Shipping in order to receive orders concerning the number of vessels to be prepared for the next voyage. Armed with this information, he was responsible for ensuring the ships were ready to sail, fully manned, fitted out and victualled for the entire trip. He was also responsible for unloading all incoming vessels and seeing their cargoes through the customs house and into the Company's warehouses.

Beneath these three was a pyramid of further specialist departments, each with a head. Some of these were: the Master Pilot, who looked after the preparation of the ships and saw them safely to their moorings and down to the sea; the Boatswain General, overseeing all the ropes and rigging; and, under him, was the 'Clarke of the Cordage'. There was a Surgeon-General, who saw to the health of the workers, as well as cutting their hair and supplying surgeons for each ship; a Purser-General, in charge of the department which handled all the money including wages for sailors and workmen; and a host of other clerks whose domains included the iron works, slaughterhouse and every other activity performed.

Although the Company began ship building by constructing a very large vessel, during the next twenty years, when over forty ships were constructed, only three more of over 1,000 tons were added to the fleet. Large ships were impressive, but they did not sail well and the cost ratio to cargo carried was not good, so by 1628 they had been completely abandoned in favour of vessels of 500–600 tons. At the same time, new laws were enacted with the intention of providing a more accurate idea of tonnage. Previously all ships had been measured on the basis of how many barrels with a capacity of 252 gallons, weighing about 2,240 lbs, could fit into the hold. Obviously there was a considerable amount of space not accounted for when using this system, so a new one was devised which used the formula: length of keel × greatest breadth × depth divided by 100 – and this forms the basic principal of the calculation used today.

During the late 1620s and through the next decade the East India Company found itself in financial difficulties and under attack from Parliament for using too much timber which might be required by the Navy. Thus, in 1639, the Company made its most momentous decision affecting its maritime concerns since the resolution to build its own ships over thirty years earlier: to close down the shipbuilding operation completely and to charter or freight all future vessels. In this way money that was tied up in ships would be available for increased trading, and private owners could bear the losses incurred by wrecks or capture by ships of Portugal or Holland, both of which were vigorously defending their East Indies trading colonies. The yards of Blackwall and Deptford were not closed, however, but hired out for repairs and refitting as well as continuing to construct small boats and to work on vessels which the Company still owned.

The outbreak of Civil War in 1642 meant that the Royal charter giving the Company the monopoly of trade in the East was worth nothing and a considerable number of London merchants who were not shareholders, known as interlopers, seized upon the chance of making a great deal of quick money by sending their own ships to India. This, together with a disproportionate number of wrecks during the years 1645–48, almost sealed the Company's fate, but in 1649, within four months of King Charles I's execution, when things looked at their blackest, seven ships sailed up the Thames. The rejoicing at Court was enormous and a special service was held at a London church for such a 'great and unexpected mercy'.

After this very difficult period, the Company's fortunes began to look up. Oliver Cromwell began badly by 'borrowing' £60,000, and in one year no ships at all were sent for the first time since 1612, but then, in 1657, he granted another charter, which gave new impetus and the Company began to grow again. In the meantime, the Blackwall yard had finally been sold to Henry Johnson, who was able to benefit from the upturn in demand by specializing in producing vessels suitable for the East India trade. It seems that the Company may have retained an interest in the yard, for in 1666 Sir Thomas Brame visited it and wrote 'Blackwall hath the largest wet dock in England, and belongs chiefly to the East India Company', and in 1747 a plan of the yard shows part of it still in the Company's keeping.

With the death of Cromwell and subsequent restoration of the monarchy in the person of Charles II, the Company bought several ships, freighted a number more and recommenced, although gingerly at first, its sailings to the East. These proved to be so successful that seven years later, in 1667, 14 ships departed and this number slowly grew until 1681 when 24 sailed. This new prosperous trade brought about an interest in territorial acquisition, which later became the Company's hallmark. It began with the renting of the Island of Bombay from the King, who had acquired it as part of the dowry brought with Catherine of Braganza, his Portuguese Queen. At the same time the nature of trade began to change: pepper and spices gave way to Indian fabrics, and tea made its first appearance. A curious Samuel Pepys wrote in 1660 of his first taste of 'China drink' and the King received some as a present in 1664. If we combine the ships owned with those freighted, the Company's fleet numbered between 30 and 40 vessels, which imported goods worth several hundred thousand pounds each year. The tables even began to turn on exports, with goods considerably exceeding cash, much to the satisfaction of the directors, who remembered the days when accusations had been levelled against the Company for denuding the country of gold and silver.

The 1670s saw continued prosperity, although there was still strong competition from the interlopers and at home all sorts of moral questions were being raised over the ethics of putting English weavers out of work through the importation of cheap Indian cloths and silk. However, with the support of Charles II and then his brother, James II, the Company managed to weather these attacks and even obtained letters patent to give it the right to confiscate the goods and ships of interlopers.

James II was the last of the Company's Royal supporters; after his flight to France in 1688, a new liberalism was born in England and the monarchy gave up its supreme prerogative. In the years following the interlopers formed themselves into an organized body and, after taking control of the Levant Company, relentlessly pressurized Parliament to wind up the Company or, at least, to end its monopoly. The end came in 1698, when the politicians proposed a low interest loan for themselves. The Company offered £70,000, but the interlopers raised £2,000,000 and so a bill was passed to form a new joint stock company. Pepys wrote (and it is an indictment of the morals of the age): 'The old East India Company lost their business against the new company by 10 votes in Parliament, so many of their friends being absent going to see a tiger baited by dogs.'

After the establishment of this new company, the old Company's stock dropped from 300 to 37, but the directors managed to save it from extinction by persuading Parliament (perhaps there was no sport that day!) to allow them to continue trading in the spirit of the new free competition. The result of all this was, of course, a glut of eastern goods on the market and falling profits for both concerns with twice as many ships sailing. In 1702 the idea of amalgamating the two was promulgated and passed. Six years later this was done and the resulting single organization began with capital of £3,200,000. In 1711 and again in 1730 the charter was renewed and extended.

The first forty years of the eighteenth century was a period of relative peace and the Company was able to strengthen itself. Exports increased to over £1,000,000 each year and sailings grew steadily from 13 in 1709–10 to 20 in 1720–21 and after that levelled out to average 15 for the next twenty years. With the capital properly organized, regular dividends of between 6% and 12% were paid and a £100 share was worth at least three times its face value and some-times as much as £500.

•   In Elizabethan days the officers of a ship were chosen by the merchant who owned the vessel and he sailed as the commander. Very often he had little or no idea of seamanship or navigation, so also on board was a master, who was in charge of the actual sailing of the ship, and a pilot, who was the navigator. When the first ships of the East India Company sailed, no one knew of any other arrangement, so James Lancaster, who had experience of a previous trip to the East Indies, was chosen as 'Generall of the Fleet'. He sailed in the *Red Dragon*, which, as the largest ship, was flagship of the expedition. The Company appointed John Middleton, who sailed in the *Hector*, 'Vice Admiral' and John Davis to be 'Pilot Major'.

Davis had considerable experience and, to use an Elizabethan expression, had 'used the sea' for many years. His qualifications included a trip to the Arctic in search of the North-West Passage and the guiding of a Dutch voyage to the East Indies. Lancaster was a ships' captain in his own right, but on each vessel was a master, six master's mates, twenty-two carpenters and caulkers, who were necessary due to the regular need for repairs, and a large number of ordinary seamen.

Later on the practice of carrying a 'Generall' faded out and each ship had a captain who was in complete command and, during the days when the Company built its own ships, there are various men-tions in the *Court Book* of men who wanted this position. In 1607 Thomas Dickhorne offered to 'adventure £550 to be master of one of the ships', but was unsuccessful. The Company had a Committee for Choice of Officers and Sailors; however, as 'committee' was used to denote a single member of the Court of Directors, there is some confusion as to whether the job was given to a group or just one man. If it was just one, he would presumably be advised by such people as the ship builder and the ship's husband. Potential officers were tested as to their abilities and experience as is shown in an entry from the *Court Book* dated 9 December 1607: 'Richard Rowles examined by Sir James Lancaster as to his fitness [and] appointed to go as chief man in the second ship.' Once the officers were chosen, they were ordered to 'stay aboard the ships day and night, to see things faithfully done', and were paid 'harbour wages' from the date of their commission together with money to hire small boats.

The choice of petty officers was probably left to the individual masters and mates, and they may have picked men with whom they had previously sailed, or listened to recommendations. There is little information as to how the ordinary seamen were found, but we can confidently assume that hopefuls would gather at the dockyard and the officers would advertise around the various places along the river where sailors congregated and any applicants would be sent to the committee for vetting. The Company took some care to ensure that these men were not too bad, although they were undoubtedly a rough, hard-drinking bunch and not a few were seeking to flee from justice. In 1608 the directors felt compelled to make the following comment: 'John Poole, victualler in Southwark, [is] desirous to go to the East Indies to defeat his creditors; neither he nor any such to be employed.' The Company had a 'Committee for Entertaining of Marriners', who preferred 'able men, unmarryed and approved saylors'. Throughout its long history the Company never had any trouble in finding sailors as it always paid more than the Navy and, despite the high mortality rate, the chance of great adventure was as good a reason as any for a young man to sign on and escape from disease ridden cities, whilst a sizeable proportion of the men who shipped out were from depressed country areas and felt inexplicably drawn to the sea. After the demise of the dockyards and the decision to freight ships was taken, the choice of commander and crew passed out of the Company's hands, although it did retain the right to refuse an officer's appointment.

Such were the risks that no merchant was prepared to put all his money into one vessel so, after the Committee of Shipping met and decided how many and what type of ships to take on for the following year, various members would go to one of the many coffee houses in London (the Jerusalem is one often mentioned), where they would meet with their friends and together decide how best to use this information to their own advantage. This generally involved forming a syndicate which would approach a ship builder, obtain a quote for the desired vessel and then, using its foreknowledge of the maximum sum the Company was prepared to pay for freight per ton, place a tender (which they knew would be accepted) together with an order to start building immediately. Later the whole operation became so smooth that offers of ships were placed at the same time as the future voyages were being discussed and the price would then be negotiated. As a rule, the shares of the ship were divided into thirty-two parts and an investor could own one or more portions which he would insure individually.

Names of the Company's directors featured as partners in virtually every ship which sailed, and gradually the Company's shareholders realized that these men were making a very substantial fortune out of this business, but were powerless to do anything about it. The 'marine interest' was so strong that its members were able to decide how much the Company would pay per ton and prevented anyone else from tendering a ship by persuading the ship builders to refuse to construct a vessel which would be offered at less than their rates. They grew so rich that they were able to own shares in an increasing number of ships and their stranglehold over the dockyards, together with the fact that there were no other ships in England which the Company found suitable, meant that their ring could never be broken.

Many of the most powerful men in the Company were involved in this scandal and they believed it to be their right – as a director's salary was a paltry £300 per annum – to make money indirectly out of the Company. Those who were involved in the marine interest were almost invariably people with a background in shipping. Some, such as Sir John Banks and Sir Josiah Child, who both served as Governors of the Company, started their careers as victuallers to the Navy, a well-known way of making a great deal of money, and then progressed to have shares in the Levant Company, in interloping ships, and finally in the East India Company. Others, especially Sir Henry Johnson (who bought the Company's yard at Blackwall), were shipbuilders or retired captains and some were rich landowners who saw an opportunity for easy profit.

Shares were saleable on the open market or transferable at death. Sir Henry Johnson left his shares to his son, who went on eventually to own ninety 'thirty-seconds' involving thirty-nine different ships. The daughters of rich businessmen married younger sons of aristocrats to the satisfaction of both parties, one acquiring a place among the nobility and the other extra wealth. Some, like Sir John Banks, bought a great estate and became a landlord, others went into Parliament, but nearly all of them were eventually related in some way.

This blatant exploitation to the detriment of the great mass of shareholders caused the Company many problems, which came to a head in the 1680s and 1690s when, during a period of low or non-existent dividends, it was revealed that the marine interest and other large shareholders (the two generally went hand in hand) were being allowed to trade on their own account in India for sums up to the amount of their stockholding on payment of a nominal 18%. This happened during the time of a cash crisis in India and ships there were lying empty and idle awaiting more sailings from London carrying cash for purchases, and many returned with spare room. It was a difficult period for the Company as the King had granted a charter to the new company and there was much competition.

After the two companies were forced to join together in 1708, one of the major reforms which was introduced at this merger was an attempt to crush the marine interest. A bylaw was passed prohibiting any director from owning shares in ships, and future vessels were to be taken up by open tender from two owners and a commander. This did not deter most of the hardened members of the marine interest, who simply transferred their shares amongst members of their families, but it did allow new owners in and dramatically reduced the discontent.

These new rules attracted many people who had hitherto been barred from investing, for there is nobody more vociferous than the man who cannot have what he wants, but these potential owners were cautious. The risks of foundering or capture were still very real and many felt themselves unable to risk their money without some form of guarantee from the Company. A loose type of precedent had been established during the 1660s, when a syndicate had been permitted to replace a ship which was captured, and this was repeated several times, but as a favour rather than a right. The new owners demanded that this become a regular convention and went even further. The Company had a rule that a vessel was 'worn out' after four voyages and refused to charter it for any more. This was said to be totally unacceptable on the grounds that an investment so large as was required to build a ship and completely fit her out could never be recouped in such a short time.

The proponents of this view had a perfectly reasonable case. The Company would only take on ships which had been built according to its own set of specifications, which demanded a craft much larger than any other type of vessel in English waters. Normally the owner of a merchant ship which was no longer strong enough for a long voyage could use it for coastal trade or short trips to Europe, but this was not the case with 'worn out' Indiamen, which were consequently claimed to be totally unsaleable. Occasionally the owners had petitioned the Company to allow them to replace an old ship with a new one and, as the Court of Directors was comprised mainly of old marine interest men, this was agreed without demur. The Company would have saved itself a considerable amount of money over the next ninety years if the decision had been taken at this time to revert to building its own ships, but with a group of directors who had a vested interest in not allowing this to happen, it is hardly surprising that they put their own considerations first.

In this way the strange system which became known as 'hereditary bottoms' was introduced. The way it worked was this: once a ship had completed its fourth voyage, the representative of the owners would approach the Company with a tender to supply another in her stead (known as replacing the bottom). This was always agreed to, even though there was nothing in writing, and one ship was said to have been built 'on another's bottom' in a type of self-perpetuation. The system was just as bad as the old one which it was meant to replace, but the Company had little choice but to accept it and it was probably only because of the greatly increased number of ships required during the eighteenth century that the new marine interest managed to escape the type of vocal criticism that had been in evidence in the 1690s. As a result of the hereditary bottom system, we can trace constantly recurring names of ships: there were nine *Britannias* altogether, four *Antelopes*, *Asias* and *Hopewells*, and many ships' names recur thrice. Some vessels were named after well-known people and their replacements can be seen to alter slightly as their namesakes advanced through various ranks of nobility: *Lord Camden* became *Earl Camden* and, finally, *Marquis Camden*.

The representative of the owner's syndicate was known as the ship's husband and, in the same way as the Company's ship's husband back in the early 1600s was responsible for provisioning the ship for sailing, this man was the only one of the owners who actually did anything towards the preparation of the vessel.

Almost without exception the husband had risen through the ranks in the Company's marine service to become a captain. Once he held this rank he was able, if his family connections did not already offer this, to meet Directors and owners whose influence would later be of great use. He also learned all the practical details of running a ship and understanding the crew. Out of his trading allowance (private trade), an ambitious captain could, after four or five voyages in command, retire with a handsome fortune, which could then be used for buying shares in ships and providing the necessary incentives to gain him a favourable position at the Court of Directors.

During the first half of the eighteenth century the shipping requirements of the Company increased considerably and the number of existing bottoms grew steadily. A retired captain with capital would join forces with a couple of major investors and answer the Company's advertisement for a new ship, offering to fulfil the role of husband. There was obviously enormous competition to gain a new bottom so a would-be husband had to be continually in touch with his friends in positions of power to find out when a likely offer was going to be made, so that he could then act quickly to find a suitable commander and put his syndicate together. It was at this stage that family connections and the hidden interests of Directors could be seen at work, as any husband who had not done his ground work properly had little chance of success no matter what he tendered. Having succeeded in winning the order, a husband was in possession of a bottom, which always belonged to him, not the other owners in the syndicate no matter how large their shares, and an order would be placed with a ship builder together with a substantial deposit. The Company laid down strict demurrage rules, which were fines for lateness in delivery or date of sailing; a ship which was very late could be cancelled and she would be said to be a lapsed bottom. The shareholders paid their capital as and when it was needed, which could be over a period of some years, so dividends would often come in before the ship was fully paid up, especially when it was common practice to 'sell the ship', i.e charge a captain for his command.

In the first part of the century there were a considerable number of husbands, but as time went by a small number of highly successful ones bought out many of the others on their retirement or death, until men such as Thomas Hall and John Durrand controlled large numbers of ships. By the 1760s it had become such big business that families became professional husbands and we see brothers Charles and John Raymond, the Moffatts and the Liells names recurring time and time again over several generations. Charles Raymond made so much money that he opened a bank and was knighted. His only daughter married the heir to a great landowning family, the Burrells, and was granted a special Royal dispensation for her father's hereditary title to pass to her son, without which it would have died out. The Burrells, of course, were also interested in the Company's shipping and had owned shares with Charles Raymond's great uncle many years earlier.

In an attempt to eradicate the seventeenth-century problem of captains who could not sail, the Company insisted that a potential commander be at least twenty-five years old and had sailed on at least three previous occasions, once as fifth or sixth mate, once as third or fourth mate and again as chief or second mate. Apart from this and the performance of appearing before the Court to take the oath, these were the only requirements. The husband and owners had complete control over who they nominated and they could do particularly well out of the practice of 'selling the ship'. This applied only to a new bottom and often cost as much as £10,000, a substantial sum, and it ensured that only the sons of affluent families could afford it, keeping the marine service very much a *corps d'élite*. One noble family which was considering sending a son to sea received the following advice from James Rennell, the famous geographer:

Of the two services [the Royal Navy and Company's marine], I should prefer the India Service for a boy at his first going to sea. He has there less chance of being corrupted than in the Navy where there is such a parcel of idle young Fellows in every ship: he will probably make a swifter progress in learning his Duty and will be much closer overlooked by the Captain, or whoever has charge of him, than the nature of the other Service will allow. . . . The Officers of India ships are known to be in general thoroughbred seamen, and are seldom refused preference in the Navy after being a very short time in it.

Another who wrote of the Company's ships said, 'Their commanders are men of superior attainments, as gentlemen and as officers.'

Once a man owned a captaincy, it was, like a bottom, a saleable asset which could be disposed of upon retirement, transferred to a member of one's family or sold by a widow in the case of a captain who died at sea. There was some agitation for a chief mate, who succeeded to the command by the unexpected death of his captain at sea, to be confirmed in this rank for the ship's next voyage, as there were a number of these men who were extremely able sailors but had no money to buy a command and, towards the end of the century, it became easier for a chief mate to borrow the money when such a thing happened.

For a man to expend such a sum there had to be a good reason and this lay in the concept of private trade. The Company paid its officers badly – a captain received £10 per month – but it did allow all the officers and petty officers some space on board ship in which they could indulge in a small amount of business on their own account without having to pay freight charges. This was private trade and in the days when the Company sent the only ships to the East it was a valuable right. It was said that it was not until a man made second mate could he live in the style of a gentleman off his salary and freight allowance, but once this rank was attained the rewards for an astute trader could be very good indeed. The captain had the largest private trade allowance, varying from 50 to 56 tons according to the size of the ship, whilst the chief mate was allowed 8 tons, the second mate and surgeon 6 tons each, and so on down to the six quarter-masters who shared between them 1.5 tons. Some sold their allocation to the captain or asked him to trade on their behalf.

There were certain limitations as to what private trade could be indulged in; for instance, ships returning from India could not bring

Chinese goods like tea and chinaware and, conversely, ships on the China run were prohibited from bringing back Indian cloth and spices. As the civilian and military population grew in India, the permanent residents clamoured for whatever English goods they could obtain and many captains made successful liaisons with local shopkeepers supplying them with the latest European fashions, which, despite being completely unsuitable for the climate, were snapped up. There even developed quite a race between captains of various ships to reach India first so that their own goods could be on the market before anyone else's. Commanders of the ships going to China would normally bring back a mixture of tea and chinaware, but others would take orders for complete dinner services to be specially painted with a coat of arms or initials, and these became great status symbols for the best houses, even though their owners might have to wait three years for delivery.

Tea was, however, the main staple of the China trade and, because of the high tax, an enormous quantity was smuggled into England. Commanders of Indiamen were often major suppliers to the smugglers and the great Georgian diarist William Hickey describes how, when he was on the *Plassey* in 1770, one came aboard and bought about 60 chests for £18 each. Upon the appearance of a customs boat, the smuggler captain coolly transferred the cargo whilst the official ship looked on helplessly as the transaction was made just outside territorial waters. Not all captains were so lucky, though, and five years later one lost his command and his fortune after being charged with smuggling. So corrupt were various members of the Court that he was able to buy back his captaincy, only to be convicted again a couple of years later and, when fined close on £100,000, escaped to India, one presumes aboard another Indiaman.

A clever captain could make as much as £10,000 per trip; there are accounts of one who made £30,000, but the norm was roughly £5–6,000. Private trade was not, however, the only money-making activity on board.

The ships had some accommodation available for passengers and a captain was able to charge and keep their passage money for himself. The principal room for passengers was the great cabin, but the captain could also divide his own cabin, a roomy affair with good ventilation called the round house, into several parts to accommodate more if he wished. The Company laid down a scale of fares for Army officers, ranging from £95 for a subaltern to £235 for a general officer. Other passengers, who may have been the Company's writers and factory staff, free merchants (those who were permitted by the Company to trade in India) or even young ladies going out in search of husbands, were forced to pay whatever the captain thought he could charge. In 1769 William Hickey paid £160 for a passage to India, but eight years later, when there was particular demand, he was forced to pay £315 and had to share a cabin with three others. All cabins were unfurnished and a passenger was expected to bring his own furniture, which he would no doubt find was rapidly eaten by woodworm in India. Colonel Alexander Champion was charged £227 for a passage home in 1764 and had a part of the round house which included 'two windows'. Hickey, on the other hand, paid over double this in 1779 for a smaller cabin and four times as much again in 1808 on his final voyage.

As regards meals, passengers could opt to sit at the captain's table, which was supplied with the best possible food and wine. In 1797 a passenger on board the *Sir Edward Hughes* described one dinner which included pea soup followed by roast leg of mutton, two chickens, two ducks, two hams, corned beef, pork pies, mutton chops, cabbages and potatoes and topped off with an enormous plum pudding. At this table sat the captain, first and second mates, all passengers of standing and any young gentlemen who were experiencing their first taste of the sea, generally under the watchful eye of the commander. Officially referred to as captain's servants, but more commonly called guinea pigs, these boys were usually eleven or twelve years old and were seeing if they liked the life; if they did, on the next voyage they would sail as midshipmen. To sit at the captain's table cost about £100 extra and anyone who could not afford this sat in the third mate's mess and ate the ordinary ship's fare.

With ten passengers outwards and five on the homeward bound trip, which was by no means uncommon, a captain could make £3,000 before his private trade was even taken into account. As the minimum profit on this was considered to be 100%, it only took an investment of £1,500 to make a total of £6,000 for the round trip, so it can be seen how a captain who had made three voyages could easily have £5,000 to spend. Not all, however, came out as rich men. Those who suffered shipwreck or capture by an enemy would loose everything and the Company had a special fund to which an impoverished officer could appeal.

Most captains made three or four voyages as a commander before retiring and selling their commission. They usually served on a number of different ships and in only rare cases are there examples of loyalty to one vessel, although a captain seems to have always been employed by the same husband. Other officers do not appear to have been so rigidly bound by this convention and examples may be found of them sailing under several husbands. The only instances of long service in one vessel or its immediate successor are in the cases of William Fitzhugh, who commanded the *Derby I* and *II* for six voyages between 1715 and his death in Calcutta in 1730; and Samuel Martin of the *Harrison* (1727–38), Henry Kent of the *Dragon* (1746–55) and Thomas Dethick of the *Griffin* (1748–61), all of whom captained their ships for four consecutive trips. There are some interesting cases of captains who transferred their rank within their families, which can be illustrated by Isaac Worth, captain of the *Houghton II* (1742–49), who succeeded his father William, who had the same appointment in the *Houghton I* between 1728 and 1740; Robert Bootle commanded the *London VI* and *VII* for a total of five voyages between 1723 and 1739, and his long-serving son Matthew, who had acted as purser for all of these trips, succeeded to the command for two voyages between 1741 and 1747. A similar example can be found in the case of Matthew and William Bookey, who between them captained the *Shaftsbury I* and *II* for six voyages, 1736–55, but the most extraordinary family of all must be the Larkins, whose members, during a period of seventy-seven years, made a total of ninety-nine voyages.

Once the captain and husband had their tender accepted, a new keel was laid at one of the dockyards along the River Thames, the most famous of which were Perry's (the old Blackwall yard), Barnard's at Deptford and Randall's at Rotherhithe. Throughout the entire process of building the new hull was kept under constant surveillance by one of the Company's officials from the master attendants office, whose job it was to ensure that the new ship conformed exactly to specification and that no unseasoned wood or shoddy workmanship was incorporated. In addition to the Company's representative, the owners also employed their own surveyor to inspect progress and all this supervision apparently caused shipwrights considerable annoyance. Strikes were not uncommon and it was said that they far preferred building ships for the Royal Navy, whose inspectors were not nearly so diligent.

During the seventeenth century vessels varied in tonnage considerably as the Company strove to find the optimum size. In 1615 the *Court Book* declared that 'ships of 300 tons at least and so forth to 600 or 700 tons were fittest . . .'. Various experiments were made with vessels of over 1,000 tons during the next ten years, but these were found to be inefficient and expensive. By the time the Company closed its own yards and resorted to freighting, the average ship was about 500 tons and this size remained fairly constant, although there were cases of vessels of 250 tons and 700 tons or more, until the tea boom occurred in the early 1680s and prompted a number of ships of between 900 and 1,300 tons to be built. This dropped dramatically as war with France claimed most of the larger ships as prizes. At the time when the Old and New Companies were amalgamated in 1708, the most popular size for a ship was between 300 and 400 tons. During the next three decades this rose to 440, then 490 and finally 498 tons by the 1740s.

The Directors then apparently remembered a clause which had first been introduced in the old charter of 1693, which declared that any ship of over 500 tons was to carry a chaplain and, in a fit of miserliness, they decided to rate all vessels at 499 tons, no matter how large they were. By 1750 most new Indiamen were probably about 600 tons or more, but they kept their 499 ton rating until 1772, when a Government inquiry into the alleged overuse of oak by the Company forced all ships to be rated at their builder's measurement. With this adjustment of sixty ships, all of which were supposedly 499 tons, forty were re-registered at between 657 and 750, eighteen were in the region of 750 to 800, and two were over 800 tons. The Company insisted on continuing with a standard chartered tonnage and at the close of the century 1,200 tons was the favourite size for a 'China ship', even though they were often substantially larger.

The owners generally paid the builder in instalments beginning with a sizeable deposit when the keel was laid and followed by three more which were timed to coincide with the completion of framing, laying of gun deck beams and the last when the upper deck timbers were in place. The hull was then kept in dry dock while teams of specialists worked on her: the caulkers filling every crevice with oakum and then sealing everything with melted pitch; the carvers decorating the stern and making the figurehead; a tin man coating the walls and ceiling of the galley with sheets of metal to reduce the risk of fire (and for a similar reason the walls of the powder room were plastered); and the painters who moved in, once everything was finished, to give a couple of coats to all the decorative features, doors and windows.

When all this was done, the new ship was launched and a banquet was usually held to celebrate. Once on the river, the Company's inspectors came down and, provided all was well, pronounced her ready. Then the iron ballast bars (kintledge) were loaded, the masts and bowsprit put in place, and the rigging installed. Fitting the masts was usually done by hauling them up from a specially adapted hulk

Admiral Thomas Griffin, after whom the ship was named.

(*Below*) Headquarters of the East India Company in Leadenhall Street, London, as they were in 1750.

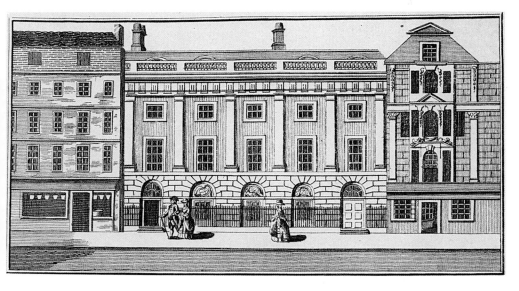

Blackwall Yard as it was when the *Griffin* was built there, with what is now the Royal Naval College, Greenwich, background left.

A modern, but historically accurate, representation of the *Griffin* moored at Whampoa, near Canton.

Three contemporary paintings of East Indiamen similar in design to the *Griffin*.

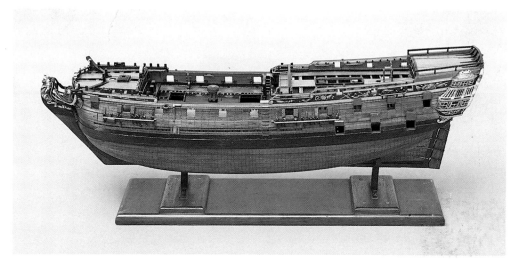

A contemporary model of the East Indiaman *Somerset* built in 1738 showing the standard design with a fo'c'sle and two after decks, whilst the plan (*below*) of the *Falmouth* shows an East Indiaman virtually identical to the *Griffin* with her deck flush from the bow to the single after deck; the *Griffin* was the first recorded Indiaman of this type.

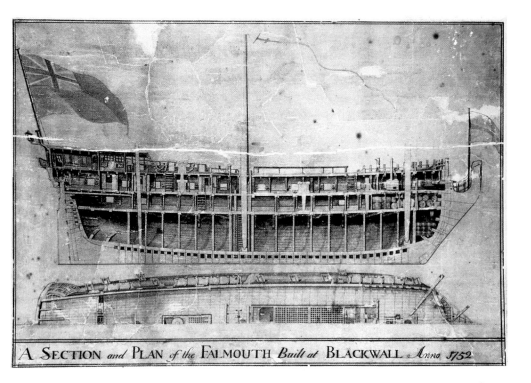

A SECTION and PLAN of the FALMOUTH Built at BLACKWALL Anno 1752

Fort St George, India, as it was when the *Griffin* called there and (*below*) a view of Fort William (Calcutta).

Two paintings from a superb set showing the entire panorama of the Pearl River at Canton *c.* 1760: (*above*) East Indiamen from various countries moored at Whampoa with their bankshalls on the shore and the customs post to the left; (*below*) the European factories at Canton, each with its flag flying.

A Chinese passage or 'chop' boat used to transport ships' officers from Whampoa to Canton.

Alexander Dalrymple.

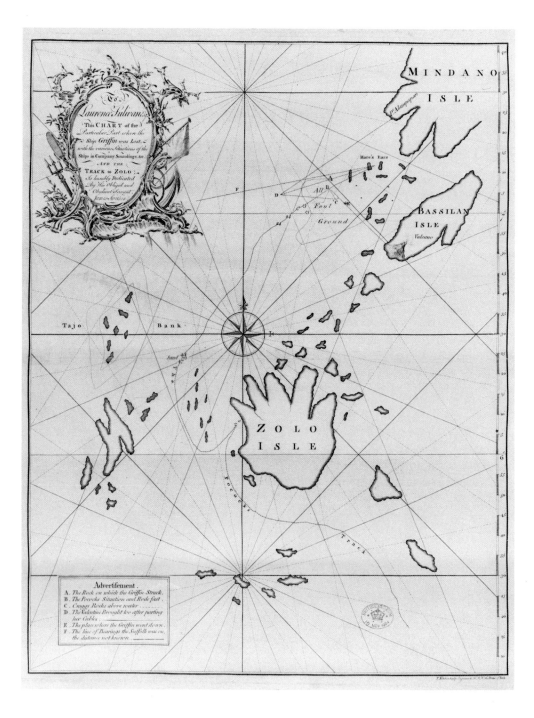

This chart drawn in 1760 by James Swithin, third mate of the *Griffin*, shows the circumstances of her loss and proved the most important key to her rediscovery.

which came alongside, but this process was considerably hastened when, in 1791, Perry's yard built a tower, which they called the mast house. A new ship was manoeuvred into position below it and the masts were simply dropped in. The rigging took four weeks or so to complete, at which time the ship was afloat and sailed down to Gravesend, where a swarm of small Company craft known as hoys stocked her with cargo, stores and provisions.

As far as the cost of constructing a ship goes, in 1607 William Burrell convinced the Company to take on their yard at Deptford with the promise of building at £5 per ton. In the years following 1640, when the first freighted ship sailed, it is difficult to discover their cost as few records of private owners survive, however, between 1670 and 1690, Thames shipbuilders were charging between £6 and £8 for men-of-war of the same size as Indiamen, so we can assume that this was a fairly constant figure as there was little difference between them.

In 1747 Samuel Braund placed an order with Perry's yard for a 499-ton vessel at £8 10s per ton, which was probably the cost of the *Griffin*, but shortly after this the price began to rise. In 1781 an 800-ton Indiaman cost £14 14s and by 1800 it had gone up to £21. Owners were nevertheless able to reap sizeable profits from the Company as freight rates were always considerably higher. In 1642 the rate was £25 per ton, but by 1715 this had slipped back, after a brief wartime rate of over £30, to £21–£24 (depending on whether the destination was the East or West Coast of India). This remained static until 1754, when it rose to £24–£27. The outbreak of the Seven Years War increased both the risk and insurance premiums, so the rate rose to £37–£40 in 1760. Twelve years later it was £34–£37, and renewed hostilities in 1780 forced it up to £47. With peace, the Company insisted that there was no reason for it not to drop back again, but this met with firm resistance from the owners, and their opposition marked the beginning of the end of the hereditary bottoms convention.

For some years a new generation of businessmen had tried to offer their ships at lower rates, but the marine interest had such influence that any new tender had always been refused by the Court of Directors. In 1785 a syndicate headed by Anthony Brough offered to supply eighty ships at £22–£24 per ton but, after his tender was accepted (in the face of strong opposition), he was thwarted by the ship builders who, bribed by the old owners, refused to build for him. There was a further disgraceful scene when, after the Committee of Shipping proposed a new rate of £31, the directors voted for £35.

Finally, the mounting tide of public opinion had gathered such a following that, on 6 February 1796, the Court passed a resolution which did away with hereditary bottoms and opened up the system to sealed public tender. At the time there were eighty-seven old bottoms, many of which could trace their predecessors back to the early days of the century. The ship built on the *Griffin*'s bottom at this date was called the *Earl Talbot*. With their demise there also came an end of the captain's right to sell his command and the Company paid out £376,505 in compensation to this group, ever mindful of the need for good officers.

Hereditary bottoms did not, however, completely disappear as it was, in some cases, a fair system. From about 1780 the Company had introduced copper sheathing on to the hulls of their vessels in an effort to prolong their life. Introduced at a time when the Royal Navy was rapidly expanding and there was a dirth of good oak in England, it was a considerable success. Indiamen could now be chartered for six and later eight or more voyages with a thorough survey at the end of the third and sixth trips. With this increased life and the added risks caused by the outbreak of the Napoleonic War, the Company decided that it was reasonable to allow an owner to replace his ship without having to tender separately as everyone else did if she was captured or lost through no fault of the captain, providing the vessel had not completed five voyages.

With loading complete at Gravesend, a special River Thames pilot was taken aboard and the ship would make her way to the Downs, where she waited for a suitable wind, often for a couple of weeks. Those passengers who could afford accommodation ashore stayed in various inns and, the day before sailing, went on board together with the ship's husband or his representative, who paid all the seamen their imprest money, or two months' wages (£5), which was all they had until they returned home again. If the voyage was to be a long one, such as to China, they would previously have been to India House to sign an affidavit allowing a nominee to collect one month's further wage for every six months' absence. There were various agents who would safely keep a single man's money; married sailors generally had theirs collected by their wives.

If a ship was captured or lost, by Act of Parliament no wages were paid at all as the basis of payment was believed to be dependent on a profitable voyage and this remained the case throughout the entire Merchant Navy until 1854. There were also severe penalties if there was the least suspicion that the vessel was carrying any smuggled goods and the entire ship's company could find their wages mulcted or reduced as a result. During the seventeenth century sailors would be paid half wages whilst the ship was still at Gravesend, however this was stopped because too many men absconded and, thereafter, money was only paid when it was too late for a sailor to leave his ship.

All Indiamen sailed between mid-December and mid-January as the winds were right to carry them past the Portuguese coast and into the mid-Atlantic. Throughout most of the seventeenth century the ships preferred to sail in a direct line for the Cape of Good Hope, so they passed close to Madeira and then stopped at St Taigo in the Cape Verde Islands for water and fresh provisions. Edward Barlow's ship, the *Experiment*, stayed there for about a week in 1670 and loaded up with hogs, goats and hens as well as sour limes, oranges, 'cokenot' and some vegetables.

The luxuries to be found on a captain's table were specially bought from private suppliers, but the provisions which were loaded on to an Indiaman for everyone else came from the Company's warehouse. Drink was the most important commodity to the average seaman and almost equal amounts of water and small (low in alcohol) beer – hence the expression for something of little consequence – were taken on board. The seamen's diet consisted mainly of salted beef or pork with peas and hard ship's biscuits (the famous hard tack). On alternate days dried fish and cheese would be served up, but this was well and truly rancid by the time a ship reached the Cape Verde Islands, so, if at all possible, a stop was very welcome and helped to stave off illness. The eighteenth-century seaman ate his food off a square wooden plate and from that we get the expression 'a square meal'.

There were also liberal quantities of strong beer and cider on board, and each man was allowed a barrel of 'strong water' or brandy. The officers had an enormous assortment of foodstuffs and drink and, in order to have fresh meat, milk and eggs, took with them a number of live animals including chickens, turkeys, pigs, goats and cattle. The poultry lived in terrible conditions in tiny coops on the poop desk, whilst the other animals seem to have wandered all over the gun or main deck. The drinking water, which everyone shared, was taken directly from the filthy, stinking River Thames and must have been horrible, but during the voyage it seems to have settled and undergone a change which apparently made it quite drinkable (except, one imagines, for the sediment) and was in great demand by homesick expatriots in India.

The watering stop at Cape Verde Islands over, the seventeenth-century ship would make its way down towards the Equator and invariably find itself becalmed for several weeks in the Doldrum Calms, which Barlow described as 'the latitude of the rains'. Englishmen were unused to the climate and, because there was no further stop until after the ship rounded the Cape of Good Hope, water was rationed to three pints a day. This, combined with salted meat and continual dampness caused by the rain, must have made the men very uncomfortable. Some relief was found in catching fresh fish, which at least supplemented their diet. Later ships, such as the *Griffin*, avoided this course and sailed with the north-east trade winds directly from the region of the Cape Verde group to the coast of Brazil, often seeing, as their first landfall, Trinidad. From there they would go down the coast and catch the westerlies as far as the tip of South Africa or, if they were too far south to see this, pick up the roaring forties and not see any land until sea birds and weed told them that the western coast of New Holland (Australia) was near, and then turn due north.

No matter what their course, sailors would always observe the ceremony of crossing the Equator. For those on their first voyage there was the choice of a fine or an indoctrination ceremony. Barlow noted in 1670 'every man who had not been so far before paying his bottle of strong waters as a forfeit'. A century later, William Hickey paid the 'customary forfeit of a gallon of rum to the ship's crew', but one of his fellow passengers could not afford this and submitted 'to the ceremony of ducking and shaving', which involved being suspended by a rope from a yard arm and being ducked three times in the sea, no doubt much to the amusement of the old salts, considerably refreshed by their strong water.

Those ships which went around the Cape of Good Hope or Cape Bonisprance as it was also known would not stop, unless there was an emergency, until the Island of Johanna, one of the Comoro group in the straights of Madagascar. Here the ships received a great welcome from the friendly islanders who had made themselves rich out of the Europeans. Both Barlow and Hickey testify to their feelings of friendship with the English Royal Family and, according to Hickey, the local King's eldest son even insisted on calling himself His Royal Highness the Prince of Wales, which he felt was a title borne by all heirs to a throne.

Some ships went instead to the Maldive Islands or even Ceylon, but by this stage in a voyage a stop was required as the dreaded scurvy had almost certainly broken out. Barlow took the possibility of contracting scurvy in his stride as a type of occupational hazard, commenting that it was a problem 'which happeneth in all ships after they come out of England and come into these changes of air and hot countries'. He and many after him assumed that the cure was simply to touch shore and rest on land for a few days. Some years later (1696), he seems to have attributed its cause to lack of water, writing: 'We had to put our men to a quart each man for twenty-four hours which was but a small quantity to poor men that eat dry biscuit and salt beef boiled in sea water, and in a hot climate, which caused men to fall down upon the scurvy, especially such people as were not used to hardship and had not known the lack of drink.' To many it was still a mystery in the 1770s even though a Scottish surgeon named James Lind had published his findings and specified lemon juice as a certain cure in 1753. Colonel Flint, a passenger on board the *Nassau* during a particularly bad outbreak in 1779, asked a sailor who appeared unaffected what method he used and received the answer, 'Grog, your honour, grog is your only.'

The other disease which killed sailors was dysentery or the bloody flux. This did not generally attack men until they had actually arrived in India or the Spice Islands. Most put it down to a mixture of drinking local water and eating 'hot country provisions'. On board their ships the sailors seem to have built up a degree of immunity to the various germs which existed in their own food and drink, which multiplied as the voyage progressed, but by the time they reached India or Java the English provisions were all consumed and so they were forced to eat local products. The resulting illness could 'killeth a lusty strong man in ten days', especially if they were at sea because the cramped conditions, continual wetness and awful smell below deck was hardly conducive to a good recovery.

Deaths at sea were a fact the Company could do nothing about. Corpses were sewn up in a piece of canvas or blanket and weighted with a couple of cannon balls and thrown overboard after a brief prayer, usually before breakfast. The sailors hated this as they were only too aware of the risks they ran and disliked the thought of being eaten by sharks and other fish, but there was little choice. Passengers and Company officials who died may have been provided with a proper coffin, but everyone knew the end result was the same. In order to guard against a ship becoming undermanned (a 499-ton ship had a regulation crew of ninety-nine), the Company always sent out too many men to compensate. If the mortality rate was especially high (as in the case of the *Drake*, which lost forty-nine out of ninety-nine men in 1739–40), Chinese or Indian sailors known as Lascars could be taken on board and had to be returned home again at the Company's expense. It was considered that it took three Lascars to do the work of one English sailor, so any ship which took them on board needed extra provisions and room for their large numbers.

Most ships went to the coast of India and traded from one port to another following the coast round from Surat to Calcutta until their ladings were complete. The passengers disembarked wherever they wished, but new ones would not normally come aboard until the vessel was at its final port of call. There were always fewer passengers going home, as the Indian climate claimed a large percentage of settlers, but those who did leave usually brought with them a sizeable fortune (and were therefore charged more) and much more luggage than the ones going out. Regulations as to luggage varied over the years, but usually allowed for somewhere between $1\frac{1}{2}$ and 5 tons per person. Sometimes this depended on the type of accommodation chosen: one man, sending his daughters to India in the great cabin, told them there was ample room for their piano, harp, two or three bureaux, several sea couches and various chairs. William Hickey, returning to England for the last time in 1808, took on board two large teak chests, a bureau, a cot, a table and a chair. Another case is recorded of a captain who nearly had a fit in India when a family attempted to load his ship with 120 pieces of luggage.

Each officer decorated his cabin as he wished and most were fairly spartan, although Hickey described the third mate's cabin on the *Plassey* in 1769, which was the finest he ever saw: 'It was painted of a light pea green, with gold beading, the bed and curtains of the richest Madras chintz, and one of the most complete dressing tables I ever saw, having every useful article on it; a beautiful bureau and bookcase, stocked with the best books and three neat mahogany chairs.'

The crew's quarters, on the other hand, were very rough and airless, having almost no ventilation whatsoever as well as being noisy and cramped. Sailors would be called to go on deck at all times of the day or night when sails needed changing and had little chance of a long uninterrupted rest. Their furniture consisted of a hammock suspended from the ceiling, which was about six feet high, and a sea chest containing their one change of clothes and other personal items. The Company provided some books and musical instruments, and later on some members of the crew formed an orchestra which played to the captain and passengers. As a result, there was always some form of music in the crew's quarters, and sea ballads and stories told over candlelight formed the sailors' entertainment.

Whether the ship had remained in Indian waters or gone on to the Far East and China or up to the Persian Gulf, the time for leaving was always between November and January. This was especially important in the case of China ships which, if they left any later than the first week of January, might miss the winds and be forced to remain at Macau for another year. The China ships would sail out of the Pearl River, which led to Canton, and make their way directly across the South China Sea to the Straits of Sincapore (where Singapore is now located) and then on towards the southern tip of India, where they might stay at Madras to pick up a convoy or make straight across the Indian Ocean to the Cape of Good Hope and up to St Helena, an island owned by the Company, at which all homeward bound ships stopped.

At St Helena there would be a well-earned rest and restocking of water, beef and vegetables. Men with scurvy would go ashore and miraculously get well again and, after a stay of between one and two weeks, the ship would once more set sail. One of the most important reasons for calling in there, apart from the re-stocking, was to discover if, during the ship's absence from home, any new wars had broken out. If so, Indiamen would often wait for a convoy to gather or some ships of the Royal Navy to appear in order to escort them home. Sometimes during the 1760s huge fleets of merchantmen would sail with men-of-war, and fifty or sixty would enter the English Channel together. In 1757 the *Griffin* waited with three other Indiamen at St Helena until a man-of-war arrived to accompany them and in the Channel '60 or 70' ships collected together.

If the situation was quiet, many ships would steer a course from St Helena towards the Ascension Islands, where they would catch turtles. Barlow often went there and described how a small group of sailors would go ashore and wait for the turtles to lay their eggs before capturing them by turning them on to their backs as they returned to the sea. Ten or twenty were taken on board, where they would live for a maximum of twenty-five days. One would be killed each day and it fed, so Barlow says, between forty and fifty men. He said turtles were 'very good refreshing victuals for the seamen: but I, for my part, never could love them, although the victuals are very good and wholesome'. The eggs, if there were any, were made into broth. If bad or uncertain news had been received at St Helena, Barlow tells us the ships 'did not touch at Ascension, not knowing who we might meet there nor what might happen'.

Eventually the Indiaman would see the tip of Cornwall and make her way to the Downs, occasionally stopping at Plymouth, where the passengers would gratefully leave. Once in the River Thames, the Company's and customs' boats would meet her and together they would head for the dock to unload. The crew would be paid off and generally took a few months holiday before making another voyage. Sometimes, much to the Company's annoyance, the Royal Navy press gangs would be waiting in the Thames estuary to take off all the fit men and occasionally the officers as well. Many Indiamen were left so poorly manned as a result of this that the Navy had to give them back a few men to sail the ship. The captain and officers would go to India House to present themselves and their logs. Commanders were strictly entreated to keep a note of any abnormalities in their charts and it was not until the 1760s that any concerted attempt was made to establish a hydrographic department. Many ships were lost or damaged by coming upon uncharted or mispositioned reefs and rocks, and, if a captain reported something unusual, other commanders were informed. The ship would have its rigging removed and masts taken out before going into dry dock and being thoroughly overhauled and repaired until about eight months later, when the whole performance would begin again.

CHAPTER 4

The Griffin

On Thursday 29 September 1748 the London *Evening Post* reported: 'Last Tuesday the *Griffin*, a new built ship for the East India Company, was launched at Blackwall, and the command given to Captain Thomas Dethick.'

After the new ship's launch there was the customary reception on board followed by dinner in the captain's round house at the stern. The *Griffin* and her sister ship, the *Boscawen*, were the first Indiamen to be constructed with what later became known as flush decks and this revolutionary design, intended to make them faster in the water, had created a great deal of interest. The fo'c'sle deck at the bow had been completely removed giving a totally flat deck from the bow to the doors leading into the quarter deck just behind the mizzen-mast. At the stern, instead of the usual two decks, there was only one and numerous critics had already looked over the ship and pronounced her unfit for such a long voyage, saying that the sea would continually break over the lower bow and flood the entire deck. Some also believed that the captain's authority would be undermined for, when the ship's wheel had been on a raised half deck, the captain and senior officers had been the only people permitted to stand upon it. Now the steerage was open to all and the captain's only retreat was the bare poop deck.

The round house, where Captain Dethick gave his dinner, was a lovely cabin, sixteen feet long and as wide as the ship with a row of windows across the stern bulkhead. In the middle of these was a door leading on to an open gallery, all beautifully carved, painted and gilded. On each side of the windows, slip doors led into an enclosed quarter gallery which the officers used as lavatories. In the centre of the cabin, which was completely lined with wooden panelling, was a large table and, around the walls were arranged comfortable armchairs, a bureau and several other pieces of furniture.

For the curious who wished to explore the new ship, this cabin made a good start. Leaving the round house, one walked along a short passage with the captain's sleeping quarters on one side and a galley and servant's cabin on the other. On emerging through double doors the entire deck was laid out before one. Within a few feet was the mizzen-mast, the shortest of the three masts, but before this, the wheel, two binnacles and a chart table were placed. Against each side stood three guns and this entire section as far as the mast was covered by a canopy which could be, but rarely was, pulled back. On one side of the doors was the bell ladder, which led up to the poop deck. This was surrounded by a high rail and, at the stern a massive solid carved board called the taffarel (taffrail) was fixed. From it hung the huge ship's lantern and a flagpole, nearly twenty feet high, projected far above.

The main deck was also enclosed by a rail for most of its length and this became higher as it approached the stern until, by the bell ladder, it was level with the rail around the poop, giving the impression that the ship's superstructure was much larger than it actually was. In bad weather solid planks called waist boards could be fixed into position along these rails so that less water washed in.

Moving forward past the wheel and mizzen-mast, the visitor saw a substantial companionway going down to the gun deck and aft or steerage cabins. On Indiamen of the old design these had been approached directly from the main deck, but on the *Griffin* their entrance was now fully enclosed. Climbing down the companionway the first view was of a passageway leading towards the stern, lined with two fixed cabins on each side, a pantry and the cuddy or officer's ward room. In the stern was the great cabin, a fine room at least the same size as the round house above and also with a row of proper windows, but no gallery. There were the same slip doors leading to quarter galleries and this was the chief accommodation for passengers, being split up with partitions if there were several or kept open if one cared to pay for the entire space.

Remaining on this deck and moving forward, one passed two rows of nine standing cabins. These were separated from each other by canvas walls which could be taken down when the ship went into action against an enemy and the order 'clear the deck' given. The light for these cabins was provided by the ports for the cannons and in several stood one of these great guns, making conditions rather cramped, especially as most measured only eight by seven feet. The four permanent cabins were occupied by the first and second mates, surgeon and purser and the others by junior officers, midshipmen and senior petty officers. Past these, approaching the bow was the long cabin where the crew slept and then, under the fo'c'sle was the cookhouse with thickly plastered walls and a large copper funnel to avoid fires, several store rooms and two bread rooms. Right in the bow a door led out on to the beakhead, a platform around the bowsprit, and the crew used this open area as their lavatory.

Another, much less elaborate companionway led down to the orlop deck, where at the stern was located the gunner's cabin and heavily reinforced powder room. Most of this deck was open for cargo, but there was also the sailmaker's room and, by the main mast, the entrance to the well, which contained the ship's two chain pumps. This went straight down to the bottom of the ship, was lined with heavy timbers to separate it from the cargo, and a glance down would determine the level of water in the bilges. Much further forward were more storerooms for the large quantity of water and beer barrels that were needed on board every Indiaman.

Upon climbing back up to the main deck, one almost immediately came across the capstan, a large wooden device looking something like a mushroom with a twenty-three-inch stem surmounted by a large domed wheel called the drumhead. When the time came to drop anchor, the sailors collected twelve long poles which were stowed nearby and inserted them into the drumhead, making it look like a spoked wheel. They could then turn it in either direction according to whether the anchors were being raised or lowered. A second capstan was installed in the crew's long room. Further forward, most of the deck between the main mast and the fore mast was taken up with the hatchways for stowing cargo. Just before the fore-mast the chimney from the cookhouse stood up rather incongruously and the open area up to the bow was covered in ropes and other equipment.

At the time the *Griffin* was being constructed England was embroiled in the War of Austrian Succession and earlier in this conflict the Company lost three ships captured by the French: the *Princess Mary*, *Anson* and *Princess Amelia*, all in 1747. Two of these were owned primarily (in other words, the signatories to the vessel's charter party) by a London merchant of Dutch extraction named Francis Salvador and a retired Company captain, Richard Micklefield, who acted as the husband. These two were major owners of ships: Micklefield since 1730, when he retired from commanding the *Marlborough*, and Salvador since 1737, when he bought a large share in the *Devonshire*. By 1747 they owned upwards of eight vessels, but had suffered from bad luck more than most. In addition to the loss of the *Princess Amelia* and *Princess Mary* to the French, they had also lost the *Northampton*, which parted company from the *Hardwicke* in March 1746 on the way home from China and was never heard of again, and also, the *Heath-cote*, which ran aground on the Island of Socatra with £47,500 of the Company's goods on board in 1747. What was even worse was that, in the ensuing inquiry, the captain of this ship was found guilty of negligence and, as a result, Micklefield and Salvador lost the right to replace her bottom.

Fortunately, in the inquiry over the loss of the *Princess Amelia*, her captain, Thomas Best, was found to have performed his duty against overwhelming odds and was honourably acquitted, so, even though the ship had been captured, her bottom was safe. Captain Micklefield was an experienced campaigner when it came to pursuing his rights with the Company and his applications for new ships to replace worn out ones go back to 1730, when he petitioned the direc-tors 'for leave to build a ship in the room of the *Marlborough* and that she may be taken up in turn'.

News of the *Princess Amelia*'s fate filtered through towards the end of 1747 and almost immediately Captain Micklefield requested per-mission to replace her with another. The Company was forced, by the Act of 1708, to acquire its ships for each season by open tender and in order to abide by the rules, but to give any new owner as little chance as possible to comply, the Directors would post their advertisements for tenders for the following year's ships in September and allow only one week for the submission of applications. The old owners, of course, had their ships already built, so for them it was no more than a formality, but it was impossible for a new owner to build an Indiaman in the three months between September and early December when they had to be ready for lading, and anyone who built one speculatively and hoped to win in the ballot could easily end up with a ship which the Company did not want, nor anyone else, as they were too big for any other purpose. No wonder we find in the *Court Book*, year after year, the statement 'And no other ships being proposed to be balloted, they were declared accord-ingly.' The ones which 'declared accordingly' matched, strangely, exactly the number which the Company had already decided to take up for the subsequent year and any new ships had long before been agreed to, although nothing to that effect was ever put in writing.

At times like this shipowners must have realized how important was the role of the husband. Some factions in the Company and several owners were complaining of the large number of ships in the service. The problem became so severe that three years later the Directors were forced to request the owners to reduce voluntarily the numbers of bottoms from sixty-five to forty-eight as many ships which had a perfect right (if it can be described as a 'right') to sail for the Company were finding themselves surplus to requirements and lying idle in the Thames for a season. The best and most successful husbands were retired captains who, during their years at sea, had learnt all there was to know about running a ship, made enough money to buy a share in one and, most important of all, had made a number of contacts within the Company hierarchy who would be useful in a crisis. Micklefield fitted all these criteria perfectly. He had gone to sea for the first time more than forty years earlier, rising to command the *Marlborough* on four voyages between 1719 and 1730. His eldest son had also spent five years in this ship and a second son, Richard, had become commander of the *Colchester*, which his father owned, from 1740 until his death at sea on the return trip from Borneo less than two years earlier in 1746.

To secure a replacement for the *Princess Amelia*, the owners needed the approval of Directors on the committee of shipping. Richard Micklefield had been at sea with the brother of one director, William Braund, during the 1720s and shortly after his retirement had teamed up in the ownership of two ships with two fellow retired captains, both of whom, by 1748, had become Directors: the *Devonshire* with Robert Hudson, and the *Princess Royal* with William Mabbott. The Company's rules stated that a Director could not be an owner of a ship, but Mabbott and Braund were both members of very important ship-owning families and no doubt they were pleased to help an old friend.

With the go ahead secured, Micklefield and Salvador placed their order for a new ship with the famous Perry yard at Blackwell and decided to name her after the illustrious naval commodore who had recently saved Fort St David from the French, Thomas Griffin. Throughout history seamen have named their vessels after heroes or the famous and the East India Company was no exception. At various times during the eighteenth century those who protected the Company's interests found themselves commemorated by ship's names and at the same time as work began on the *Griffin*, Perry's laid down another keel for a new Indiaman which was to be named *Boscawen* after the Admiral who relieved Commodore Griffin in 1748, although at the time the two ships were started he was still serving with Anson (who also had a ship named after him) in the South Atlantic and had not reached India.

When a contract was signed, the normal terms of business provided for a sizeable deposit: at Perry's the norm was £1,000. The cost of building in early 1748 was £8 10s per ton so the total cost of the *Griffin*, which, despite the fact that the Company took her up at 499 tons, was likely to have been around 600 tons, was in the region of £5,100. Further payments were made when agreed stages of construction were completed and the balance was due when the ship was ready to take on its cargo. In addition to the actual price of building the hull, the masts and rigging had to be paid for together with the stores and supplies which could easily account for a further £15,000, making the total around £20,000. The Company advanced owners some money on account and paid the sailors' initial imprest money before the vessel sailed. Once the ship had departed there were no additional expenses until it returned and had to be repaired and refitted.

As the ballot for the following year did not occur until September, work progressed on the *Griffin* with no more than a handshake as guarantee. If we assume that her keel was laid down in January, the major building work would have been completed by the end of May. After this the deck timbers which, in contrast to the remainder of the ship, were made of pine, were put in place and then tests in the wet dock began. Apart from the deck, about 90% of the timbers were oak and many contracts stipulated that the trees must be grown in the south of England as these were considered to produce the best wood. Some elm was used and everything was pegged, rather than nailed, together using wooden pins called treenails; most contemporary accounts say that these were made of oak taken from the upper parts of the tree where sap did not run. By about June the ship was back in the dry dock and all the finishing touches were added. When everything was completed to the owner's satisfaction, the *Griffin* was officially launched on 27 September.

Less than a week before, on 21 September, the Company had

Resolved that the following publication be affixed upon the Royal Exchange and this House by the Secretary, viz: The Court of Directors of the United Company of Merchants of England Trading to the East Indies do hereby give notice that they are ready to receive Proposals at any time on or before Wednesday, the 25th day of this Instant September from any person on what Terms and conditions they are willing to let their ships to the Company for all parts of the East Indies for this ensuing Season, each Proposal being made by two of the Owners and the Captain in writing expressing therein the names of all the owners and that the same be severally sealed up and left with the Secretary, in order to be laid before the said Court.

The day after the *Griffin* was launched all the tenders were opened and read. The Committee of Shipping had already met some months previously to decide whether it would offer any increased charter rate and had decided to pay only last season's rate. It was no coincidence that all the tendering owners offered their vessels at a rate of £26 outwardbound and £29 homewardbound for the Coast and Bay (the Coromandel Coast and Bay of Bengal) and £28 and £31 for Bombay. The Directors added, 'And to China and other places in proportion with Ingress and Demorage [demurrage] answerable thereto', together with, in the light of the recent peace treaty, 'And if a war should be renewed before the said ships last departure from England, the Company to make adequate allowance to the owners for all extraordinary charges occasioned thereby.'

All together there were twenty-one ships' tenders read. Most had just returned from the East and could not be made ready to sail again in time, but the owners offered them anyway in the belief that it gave them an improved chance of being selected later if any extra ships were required, as was often the case. The name of the '*Griffin*, 499 tons, Captain Thomas Dethick' appears towards the bottom of this list, but below her are three new ships which had captains but were not yet named. This generally meant they were replacements for Indiamen which were worn out, but had not been launched, so stood little hope in the first ballot but might be taken up later. The fact that the *Griffin* was listed by name, even though she was a new ship, indicated that she was assured of success in the ballot.

Whilst the *Griffin* was under construction, both Richard Micklefield and Francis Salvador had been busy, not only watching and checking the progress and quality of her construction but also finding the crew, officers and, most important of all, a captain. In normal circumstances a vessel such as the *Griffin*, which was being built under the hereditary bottom scheme, would already have a captain in the person of the commander of the worn out ship, but as Captain Thomas Best of the *Princess Amelia* was a prisoner of the French with an unknown date of release this option was closed. As with everything else concerning the Company's marine service, contacts and prior knowledge were invaluable to the owners. A husband could not successfully tender for a ship unless he had a captain who was acceptable to the Company, whilst a potential captain could only succeed to a command when he found a husband who needed him. Generally, however, there were many more hopeful captains than needy husbands and a large number of officers who were well qualified made numerous voyages as chief mate without ever finding promotion.

Thomas Dethick, their choice, came from an East India Company family and was admirably suited to the position in every way. One of his ancestors, Sir John Dethick, had been a Director of the Company during the mid-seventeenth century and another, also Thomas, had for many years been the Company's agent in the important Italian trading city of Leghorn. He grew up near the Company's yard at Blackwall in a house which was given to his ancestor Sir Gilbert Dethick by Henry VIII and was well used to the sight of Indiamen and must have known a number of captains as a boy.

Thomas Dethick first went to sea as a midshipman on board the *Grantham* under Captain Roger Hale in 1739. He was one of the last group of potential senior officers who avoided having to spend his first voyage as a captain's or chief mate's servant as this tradition, which became a prerequisite a few years later, was at this time in its infancy. He spent nineteen months on the *Grantham*, travelling to Fort St George and Bengal and, upon his return, was paid the seemingly tiny sum of £19, but from this the purser deducted £2 for the 'hier of a man', who must have been a sailor Dethick appointed as his servant. His is the only instance the author has ever seen of a midshipman with a deduction for this.

Sea life obviously agreed with him because, for his next trip, he jumped a rank to be promoted fifth mate on board the *Northampton*. This ship was owned by Francis Salvador and Richard Micklefield and was commanded by one of their most experienced captains, Duncomb Backwell. To secure his post in this ship some family influence may have been used, as one of Dethick's cousins, Mary, was married to Captain John Stevens, the commander of another of Salvador's ships, the *Godolphin*, and young Thomas, just returned from one trip, may easily have been introduced to either Salvador or Captain Backwell by his relative.

The *Northampton* sailed directly to China between 1741 and 1742 and during the voyage the fourth mate, George Thornton, died, so Thomas was promoted in his place and this valuable experience gained him another leap-frog promotion to third mate on board his next ship, the *St George*, which spent the years 1743 to 1745 sailing around the coast of India from Surat and Bombay to Calcutta. Dethick then progressed to be second mate of the *Lynn* under Captain Charles Gilbert.

During this voyage, which took him to India and China, he became friends with the chief mate, Abraham Dominicus, who was almost unique in the Company's service in that he had begun his career as a ship's carpenter on board the *Harrington* in 1735 and had been promoted from the ranks. After the *Lynn*'s return to England in 1747, he was confirmed in the chief mate's position of another ship, but took up Thomas Dethick's offer of a place on the *Griffin* and then became captain of the *Delaware* in 1751. His untimely death in 1753 robbed him of a brilliant career, as he must have been an outstanding sailor. Also sailing on the *Lynn*, as a midshipman, was Charles Hudson.

Thomas Dethick and Charles Hudson grew up together and must have been firm friends. Thomas almost certainly secured him the midshipman's position and then, when he became captain of the *Griffin* and was free to choose his own officers, took his friend with him. It is rare to find a man who made four voyages as chief mate, but Hudson did so before he was able to secure the command of the *Talbot* once Thomas Dethick retired.

The Hudsons were an old family who rose to prominence during the mid-seventeenth century by their support for the Royalist cause during the Civil War. Henry Hudson was a rich barrister and was created a baronet by Charles ii in 1660, only a few weeks after his return to England from exile in France. His son inherited the title and had a number of children, the fourth son being christened Skeffington. In common with many other younger sons, this young man decided to pursue an academic career and eventually became the schoolmaster of the East India Company's school at Blackwall, located virtually adjacent to the Dethick mansion. Time went by and his son Charles became an officer in the Company's marine service, following in the footsteps of his neighbour's son Thomas. Then, by a strange twist of fate, his elder brother's grandson, the fourth baronet, died without an heir and, in 1752, Skeffington Hudson found himself a baronet. Charles Hudson, heir to the title, was away at sea on the *Griffin* at that time and was again away when he inherited the title in 1760 and so it was not until he returned to England as a shipwrecked sailor some eighteen months later that he discovered he had become Sir Charles Hudson.

A number of aristocratic and landed families sent their younger sons to sea, and several officers in the Company's service were either created baronets or inherited baronetcies after their sea days were over. Sir Charles Hudson holds the distinction of being the only baronet to command a Company ship whilst actually in possession of the title. He died in 1773 and was succeeded by his son Charles, who had also become a sailor in the Company's marine service. He died at sea in 1780 whilst second mate of the *Duke of Kingston* and the title became extinct as there were no other male heirs.

By 1747 Thomas Dethick had had a somewhat fortunate career. Many junior officers did not change their ships as often as he did, preferring to learn from one captain in the hope of eventually obtaining a command from the owners of the ship in which they had always sailed. If Thomas Dethick had followed this career path, he would almost certainly not have become the *Griffin*'s captain but instead ended up in a watery grave. During the eighteenth century the Company's ships made a total of 2,092 separate voyages to the East Indies. These were made by 623 different vessels, of which 123 were lost by sinking or capture. These facts produce two interesting statistics for the probability of being on board or owning a ship which was lost during that century. If we act on the premise that each ship which was lost counted for one voyage out of the total, then the chance of that individual voyage becoming a casualty was only 5.8%, but if the number of ships used is weighed against the number lost, then the possibility of each vessel becoming a wreck is a remarkable 19.7% or nearly one in five.

Thomas Dethick had no way of knowing these figures but, had he remained in his first ship, the *Grantham*, he might easily have died when she sank on her next voyage in 1741. Similarly, if his third voyage had not been on board the *St George*, but instead on the *Northampton*, on which he spent his second, then he would definitely have perished when she parted company from the *Hardwicke* in early 1746 never to be seen again. Of the officers Dethick had known from this trip, three, including the captain and chief mate, were still serving and disappeared with the *Northampton*. The *St George* lived out her full allowance of four voyages and was retired, but the *Lynn* also became a statistic when she sank on her next voyage, going down in a storm whilst moored in the river near Calcutta. Her old captain had retired, the chief and second mates (Dominicus and Dethick) had gone to the *Griffin* and the new captain was William Edgerton, who had sailed as fourth mate. He was one of the few exceptions to the Company's rule that a commander must have made a voyage as chief or second mate.

When, in later life, Thomas Dethick reflected on his career, it must have been a sobering thought to consider that, of the six ships in which he had sailed, four had sunk and he had narrowly missed three of these.

After the *Lynn*'s return from China, Thomas Dethick was now qualified, in the Company's eyes, to become a captain. He must have rejoiced when Richard Micklefield approached him with the offer of commanding the *Griffin* and presumably his family were pleased to provide the money for the purchase of this rank, as there are no records of his having borrowed the necessary sum as some captains did against the security of their own income from private trade. Before the ship was launched all the formalities of his appointment were completed and he then became busy finding the officers and crew. He approached Abraham Dominicus, who agreed to sail as chief mate, and offered Charles Hudson the fourth mate's position. Perhaps with his chief's advice, he then went back to the *Lynn* and asked that ship's surgeon, John Harvie, to join him. The third mate, Francis Robertson had previously sailed in the *Drake* and the two junior officers, Edward Bootles and James Moffat, were newly promoted from midshipmen. Moffat was a member of a powerful Company family which sent many sons to sea over several generations before giving them positions as owners or husbands, and becoming involved with them would certainly do Thomas Dethick no harm.

The *Griffin* was launched on 27 September 1748, but still required numerous small finishing touches and remained in Perry's wet dock until 11 November. On this date the captain's clerk, John Pye, began his log with the entry: 'Came out of Blackwall Dock and made fast to the Upper Moorings alongside the *Britannia*.' The next day the riggers began their work, getting the 'lower mast' into position. They continued working on various masts, yards, bowsprit and sails for another two weeks, during which time most of the sailors were signed on board and the task of loading the ship with cargo and stores began. It was the chief mate's job to supervise all this and to receive the cargo, which comprised lead and wool, and although the captain would come and go, he did not officially come aboard until the ship was in the Downs ready to sail.

On 2 December the Thames pilot, Mr Bromfield came aboard but, due to poor weather, they were not able to sail to Gravesend for four days. Once safely anchored there, the surgeon sent his medicine chests aboard, the guns arrived together with a quantity of powder and forty tons of cannon balls, and the Royal Navy sent a special mast aboard with a request it be unloaded in India for one of its vessels there. The weather continued to cause problems and on the night of the 17th a trading ship bound for the Caribbean broke loose from its moorings and collided with the *Griffin*, destroying the starboard quarter gallery. This was soon repaired and on Christmas Day the Company sent on board its most valuable cargo, sixty chests of 'treasure' or silver coinage. Each of these contained the standard weight of specie, '290 lbs 8 oz' or 2,648 ounces which, when multiplied by sixty tells us that the *Griffin* had over 278,000 ounces of silver on board for trading and maintaining the Company's affairs in India and China. The Company calculated that the *Griffin*'s cargo was worth

£78,584 and by so doing, has provided an opportunity to consider the relative value of money then and now, as the silver she carried would alone be worth about £1 million today.

The next day the officers checked the ballast and decided to take on an extra twenty tons, making the draught at the bow 17′ 2″ and 17′ 4″ at the stern. As the *Griffin* had never before sailed in a heavy swell or a storm, the correct disposition of ballast was unknown and the knowledge and experience of the officers was vital at this stage, as the wrong apportionment of ballast could cause the ship to founder. The 27th of December was also a busy day as the captain came on board and paid the crew two months' advance wages. Later all the livestock arrived together with their hay and corn, which had to be stowed away, and whilst this was going on two seamen, Thomas Bartram and John Orange, had an argument during which, according to the ship's log, 'the former stabbed the latter with a knife in the lower part of his belly of which he died in about four hours afterwards'.

Gradually the *Griffin* went further down the Thames until, on 5 January, she arrived in the Margate road. Two days later the supra-cargoes John Searle and Francis Kinnersley came on board and were saluted with nine guns. Before the mid-1750s, when the Chinese would not permit any Europeans to remain in Canton or any other part of China once the ships had departed, the merchants were taken out on each China ship and had to do the best business they could in the short time available.

From Margate to the Downs another pilot was taken on board and once there the final dispatches and letters for people in India were brought to the ship. If any passengers were going out, they too would come aboard, but on this occasion Thomas Dethick was unlucky and could not sell any spaces at his table whatsoever. The Downs marked the place of final departure from England and once a ship had sailed from there, her journey was said to have begun. According to her charter party, the *Griffin* was to be in the Downs and ready to sail from 1 December, but ships always ran late and it was more often the captains who grew angry at the delays rather than the Company. The *Griffin*, together with three other Indiamen and three Dutch ships, was forced by strong gales to remain in the Downs for a week. Several times the ship was unmoored and sails set, but a resurgence of the west wind prevented any progress. Finally, on 27 January 1749, nearly two months late, the wind came round and John Pye was able to write a heading in his log: 'Towards Fort St David'.

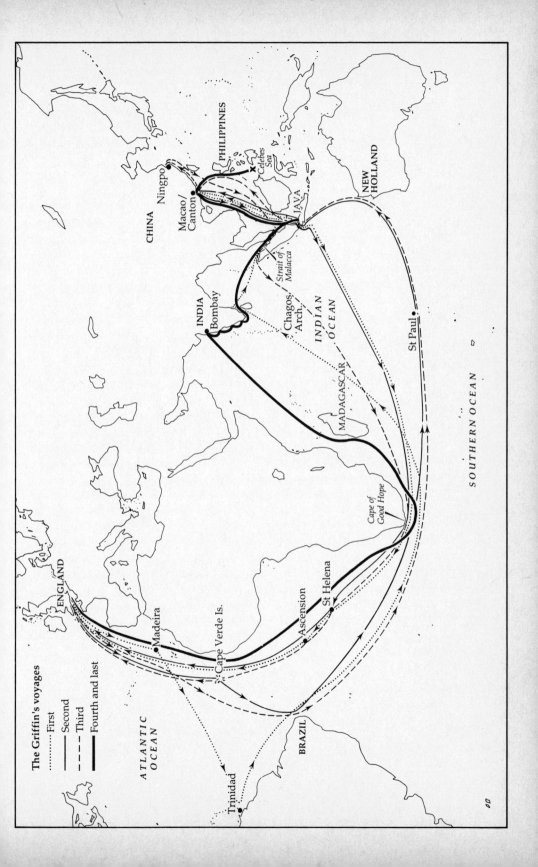

The Griffin's voyages
.... First
———— Second
– – – – Third
■■■■ Fourth and last

ATLANTIC OCEAN

ENGLAND
Madeira
Cape Verde Is.
Ascension
St Helena
Trinidad
BRAZIL

Cape of
Good Hope

CHINA
Ningpo
Macao/
Canton
PHILIPPINES
Celebes
Sea
JAVA
Strait of
Malacca

INDIA
Bombay

Chagos
Arch.

INDIAN
OCEAN

MADAGASCAR

St Paul

NEW
HOLLAND

SOUTHERN OCEAN

The ship sailed without any apparent problems or leaks other than the wedges, which held the main mast in position, coming loose and being hammered back in place. On 10 February they sighted Madeira and three days later Palma. Then the ship turned to a more westerly course for the coast of Brazil. Driven by the favourable north-east trade winds, they sailed for over five weeks without hindrance until, on 22 March, Trinidad was sighted. The *Griffin* then turned almost due south and began the long journey down the coast of South America. For Thomas Dethick this was such a standard journey that he did not mention any sightings of the coast for over two months, so whether they sailed within sight of land or not is unknown.

One aspect of the journey which did interest the captain, and the captains of all Indiamen, was anything that appeared at all unusual or did not agree with the pilot books they carried. To this extent all Indiamen were in some way on voyages of discovery because the pilots and charts were so inaccurate that each captain was charged by the Company to make a careful note of irregularities.

Finally on 24 May, after passing out of sight of the Cape of Good Hope, the *Griffin* arrived in the region of the Chagos Archipelago. During the late afternoon they saw an island which could not be readily identified so the ship stood off all night and sounded at regular intervals in case they drifted on to a reef or the shore. The next day several other smaller islands were seen and lookouts were kept at the bow and on the main mast as a precaution against suddenly coming into shallow water. Thomas Dethick thought that they were probably somewhere in the Chagos, but wrote in the log, 'We were dubious on account of the latitude, but as the latitude of them differs a degree on different drafts [charts], we judged it was not well known.' Later on the longboat was lowered and sent out in front of the *Griffin* to feel the way and by this method the ship was guided into deep water. Dethick became convinced (correctly) of the ship's position and duly reported: 'By our variation, I judge them to be a great deal more easterly than they are reported to be'. This information would eventually be reported to the compilers of Thornton's *English Pilot*, the standard guide for captains at that time and, if other commanders reported the same variation, the book's next edition would either be changed or carry a footnote explaining the possible irregularity.

A few days later they had sailed through the Maldive Islands, 'judging it better to hazard making the Moldavies [*sic*] than to lose our passage by being too far to the eastward', and were keeping a good look out for Ceylon. The weather became very stormy and Dethick wrote: 'I am afraid we are to the eastward of Ceylon, but in case we should not [be], don't care to make better than a NNW course if the wind would permit, till we are in the latitude of Cape Comorine, lest being to the West, we should miss that.'

In this haphazard fashion they sailed on until early on the morning of 14 June they spied seven or eight English men-of-war at anchor and realized that they had safely reached Fort St David, four and a half months after leaving England and without any stops.

The ships were those of Admiral Boscawen and were remaining in Indian waters despite news of the peace treaty which had been heard the previous December. The Company had two major settlements on the Carnatic coast, of which Fort St George, Madras, the main one, had been captured in the early part of the war and the survivors had fled to Fort St David 125 miles down the coast. This had held out against a long siege, thanks mainly to the ships of Commodore Griffin and the resistance of two soldiers, Robert Clive and Major Stringer Lawrence. The *Griffin*'s captain would certainly have dined most days with the senior factors here and would quite probably have met these two legendary figures during his stay.

Fort St David seems to have recovered quickly from the effects of the French siege and was operating under the premise business as usual. Once anchored, the *Griffin* unloaded thirty-five chests of her treasure together with most of the other cargo and took on board a substantial quantity of beef, water and other stores. For the two weeks this took, the captain and supracargoes lived on shore, staying at the factory or possibly in a house which may have been rented on a long lease by a number of commanders acting together. Some captains who sailed mainly to India kept permanent establishments with servants and carriages at such places as Calcutta or Bombay. The captain of an Indiaman ranked on shore as a colonel and member of the council. Whenever he landed, a thirteen-gun salute was fired in his honour and each time he entered or left a fort the guard would turn out. Captain Dethick must have been busy whilst the *Griffin* was at Fort St David, as he had loaded five chests of his own treasure and some other goods on board in London and took off two of these for purchasing Indian goods, which may have been cloth or possibly spices.

On 28 June the Griffin left Fort St David and sailed in company with another Indiaman, the *Rhoda*, for China. Ten days later they saw part of Sumatra and, at the end of July, anchored in the Straits of Malacca outside the Dutch settlement of Batavia. More water and ballast were taken on board and Dethick was forced to use his disciplinary powers for the first time when punishing Thomas Cook, a seaman who was caught 'jumping on John Clarke's belly and threatening to knock his brains out'. The sentence was thirty-nine lashes, but this was reduced ('I forgave him the rest') when he informed against another sailor who had thrown a quantity of fresh meat overboard several days earlier. This man was tried on the spot and, upon admitting his crime, received twenty-four lashes with a cat-o'-nine-tails.

A few days later a privately owned English ship which was based permanently in India (known as a country vessel) was reported to be in the straits *en route* to Manila. The Indiamen knew that the Dutch authorities intended to seize the ship if she called in to Batavia, so word was sent out advising her to anchor a considerable distance off shore. On 1 August the *Griffin* and *Rhoda*, together with the *Royal Duke*, sailed away and met with the Manila ship, which was waiting for them to bring water. The next day they separated and Dethick was asked by the other captains to lead the way through the Straits of Sincapore as they had never sailed to China before.

This course successfully negotiated, they came out into open sea and headed directly for China. On 18 August they passed over the Macclesfied Shoal, which every ship looked for to confirm her course, and on the 27th anchored at Macau, where the supracargoes disembarked.

The chief reason for sailing to China was tea, which had become so popular in England that its consumption had developed into almost a national pastime. Each Indiaman was laden with upwards of 3,000 chests of different types weighing about 400,000 lbs in total, but due to the fact that this was a light weight cargo, chinaware had initially been purchased to augment the ballast. So, because of its weight, the chinaware was packed into cases and distributed evenly along the full length of the hold just above the level of the ballast. The first consignment arrived on 15 October, six weeks after the *Griffin* arrived at Whampoa, but it was another month before a second load arrived. After that chests of tea arrived regularly and the crew were fully occupied storing it away or dealing with the large quantity of food which was also coming down from Canton. This consisted mainly of beef and pork, but also included rice and dried vegetables.

On 22 December lading was complete and the ship was cleared of all extraneous material and prepared for sailing. The supracargoes came on board with their goods and samples of next year's orders of chinaware in the evening, but returned to Canton in order to obtain the grand chop from the *hoppo*. This was obtained on Christmas Eve and the next day the *Griffin* cleared the first and second bars and anchored in the Bogue. Two days later she set sail and John Pye made a new heading in the log: 'Towards England'.

The 1749–50 season in Canton was unusual in that the Chinese discovered that one of the ships, which was probably a country vessel, had brought in some opium from India and had offered it for sale. This was only the second occasion on which the drug had been imported; the first was in 1733 on board the Indiaman *Windham* and the Chinese had threatened to seize the ship, its cargo and put to death any person who purchased it. As a result of this, the Company, who had never authorized the transportation of opium, absolutely prohibited it in any of their ships.

The return journey, which took the *Griffin* back through the South China Sea, into the Straits of Sunda, which lie between the islands of Sumatra and Java, and across the Indian Ocean, would have been completely uneventful had it not been for sighting a French ship which bore down on them on 15 March, after being first spotted over a month earlier. England and France were at peace at this date, but, as far as Thomas Dethick was concerned, hostilities could have broken out again and he would have had no way of knowing, or the ship could have been a privateer. No matter what she was, he was not going to take a chance, so he ordered the decks cleared and all the cannons primed for action. The *Griffin* hauled around and prepared for a fight, but, when the French ship was a mile away, she too hauled up and retreated, perhaps making the common mistake of believing the Indiaman was a man-of-war. The next day the *Griffin* outsailed her and successfully rounded the Cape of Good Hope on 19 March. The chase had taken them all the way across the Indian Ocean.

The *Griffin*'s first stop was at St Helena. It was an inhospitable spot, but fulfilled an important function as a place to cure sick sailors, to load fresh water and food, and had a small permanent garrison. Many years later, when Charles Hudson commanded the *Talbot*, that ship's trip from India to St Helena was so rough that all the passengers landed and refused to board again saying they would prefer to wait for another vessel. The *Griffin* arrived on 3 April, having first undergone a thorough clean and having had her sides freshly tarred. During the next nine days the crew had a good rest on shore, more water, live cattle and a passenger, Mr Sewell, was taken on board and the Captain entertained the Governor and his family to dinner. They sailed away on 13 April and headed for Ascension Island, where the crew caught some turtles, which were eaten over the next week or two.

It was six weeks' sail from St Helena to England and at 4 a.m. on 3 June the anxious lookouts were rewarded with their first view of Portland Bill. A couple of days later the *Griffin* anchored at Dover to find that the *Royal Duke*, which had also been in China, had just beaten them back. Later they headed for the Thames estuary and moored at Gravesend on the 10th, moving up to Longreach the next day, where she was met by the Company's officials and unloading began. The captain and chief mate went from there to India House, where they delivered their reports on the voyage and lists of cargo and private trade to the Committee of Shipping.

It had been a remarkably uneventful voyage. The *Griffin* had been away from home for exactly 500 days and during that time only two men had died, four had 'run' or deserted, and two were whipped. A French ship had been outrun, and both the ship and cargo had arrived undamaged. The Company and her owners had every reason to be well satisfied with the *Griffin*'s first voyage.

After the captain disembarked a flotilla of small Company river-boats known as lighters descended on the ship and spent the next week taking off her twenty-six guns, some of the cargo and all the empty water and beer casks. She was then higher in the water and was moved up to Blackwall, where, for another month, the lighters came every day to unload the tea. On 21 July the customs officers came on board with representatives of the Company and officially cleared the ship. This declaration marked the end of the charter and the crew was discharged. The *Griffin* then moved into Perry's Yard for refitting before the next voyage.

If we look at memoirs and letters written by sailors in the Company's service, most of them, at the end of a voyage, spent some time in London before returning to their families in country areas. Many found, however, that their experiences in the Far East and constantly being active made them feel unsettled and alienated once they were home. The money they received from the Company at the end of a voyage made them comparatively rich, which created some animosity, so it was not long before they returned to London or Bristol, or another port, and went back to sea. Some signed on for another Company voyage to the East, others joined or were press-ganged into the Royal Navy, whilst some filled in time between sailings to India or China by taking a short duration voyage to a European destination or even going on board a fishing vessel. For the officers life was somewhat different and most tended to stay in London, where their families had a house, and enjoy the many distractions open to a young wealthy man. Some, like Charles Hudson, were already married, but others, such as Thomas Dethick, joined in all the entertainment available.

The *Griffin* was not put forward for the Company's ballot for the 1751 season as she returned too late in 1750 to be seriously considered, so it was not until August 1752 that her name could be entered for the next lottery. In the meantime, Captain Richard Micklefield, her husband, had retired from active life and sold his shares, position and ownership of the bottoms of three ships, the *Griffin*, *Walpole* and *Marlborough*.

In 1750 and 1751 the owners had been forced to agree to reduce the number of bottoms from sixty-five to forty eight. Captain Micklefield had suffered considerably as a result of this decision because his ship *Colchester* completed her fourth voyage in 1751 and the bottom was cancelled, as was that of the *Duke of Cumberland*, which was wrecked in 1750. His career as a husband had not been particularly successful because a high percentage of his vessels had been lost and his son had died at sea in 1746 whilst captain of the *Colchester*. Without an heir, he handed over his interests to the man who had succeeded him as commander of his last ship, the *Marlborough*, Captain Thomas Hunt, and it was he and Francis Salvador who, together with Thomas Dethick, signed the tender for the *Griffin* late in 1752.

As expected, the *Griffin* was successful in the ballot and was taken up by the Company for the 1753 season and the task of finding a crew began. From her previous voyage, the chief mate, Abraham Dominicus, had been given command of the *Delaware* and had sailed for India the year before; the old second mate, John Harvey, had completely disappeared and did not reappear until 1754, when he was appointed chief in the *Prince Henry*. The third mate, Francis Robinson, had joined the *Triton*, whilst James Moffat, fifth mate, had sailed again within three months of returning to England as third mate on board a new ship, the *Warwick*. Some officers did remain with the *Griffin*: Charles Hudson, the old fourth mate, was promoted chief; Robert Dominicus, who had previously been his father's servant was made a midshipman; surgeon John Harvie and purser Thomas Lockhart signed on again; and a midshipman from the previous voyage, James Griffiths, became the new sixth mate. This left the positions of second, third, fourth and fifth mates vacant and these were filled by George Kent, Thomas Howe (who was the brother of Admiral Lord Howe), Samuel Davis and John Parslow. The fact that half the ship's officers had already sailed on the *Griffin* is remarkable considering the long break between voyages and can only be explained by the unusually smooth previous passage and Thomas Dethick's leadership.

None of the sailors could be expected to have been inactive for nearly two and a half years, but one quartermaster from 1750, Edward Tichburne, signed on again and Edward Beardmore, who may have been employed as a servant in the Dethick household, went for the second time as captain's steward.

The second voyage began in the very much the same way as the first. The *Griffin* was hauled out of dry dock on 9 October and was again secured to the upper moorings while the cargo of lead and wool was loaded. On 29 October the pilot, Mr Bromfield, came on board again and took her down to Gravesend, where she found three other Indiamen, the *Walpole*, *Dragon* and *Swallow*, already anchored. A few days later they were joined by four more: the *Boscawen*, *Suffolk*, *Edgbaston* and *Clinton*. A month later lading was completed with the arrival of forty chests of treasure and on 1 December the new husband, Captain Hunt, came on board and paid the men their two months' imprest money. From there the *Griffin* sailed down river and came to anchor near Margate on the 9th.

For this voyage there were three passengers and three supracargoes, and they joined the ship here, though they must have wished they had waited a little longer as bad weather kept the ship immobile for the next week. Whether the captain suggested they disembark and go to Portsmouth is unrecorded. Finally the *Griffin* came into the Downs, but the weather again delayed sailing and it was not until the 29th that she was able to weigh anchor and sail past Portland Bill, the Eddystone Lighthouse and into the Atlantic.

All went well and the wind carried the ship for the first 2,500 miles to the Cape Verde Islands in fourteen days, but then, once she had altered her course towards South America, the first of a series of small incidents which were to mar the entire voyage occurred. On 13 January 1753 the captain was forced to whip a man who was found below deck playing cards when he should have been on watch, and then, a few days later, a midshipman reported that some cheese had gone missing. A thorough search of the ship eventually located it, wedged between decks. These were minor incidents, but the officers realized how much the men objected to having their chests turned out and a thief on board a ship of that size, which was not due to touch land for many months, could cause morale to drop as the gossip pointed the finger of suspicion around.

At the end of January a lookout was posted for Trinidad, but after two days no land was sighted, so the captain decided to turn the ship south, thinking he might be too far to the north. Two weeks later, William Davidson, a quartermaster fell overboard during a squall and because of the strong wind it was impossible to turn the ship around to search for him. He was Thomas Dethick's first casualty through mishap.

There was more thieving towards the end of February. On the 21st, Moses Hastings, a seaman, stole five bottles of wine from two different places and admitted to part, but not all, of the theft and received fifteen lashes. The next day the log reported that they 'found the gunner's boy had stolen the money and other things we had missed . . . and, on his confession, tied him to a gun and gave him twelve lashes with a cat-o'-nine-tails'. A week later, one of the midshipmen complained that over £13, a princely sum, had gone missing. The gunner's boy was tried and confessed, and given a total of two dozen lashes over two days, but steadfastly refused to reveal where he had hidden the money.

The *Griffin*, carried by the roaring forties, headed swiftly towards Australia and on 30 March they saw the island of St Paul, which is almost 3,750 miles due south of India. Had the Griffin not been headed directly for China, she would have turned north at this point, but she continued on the same course and two weeks later 'a hawk which I imagine was blown off the coast of New Holland flew on board'. They turned north and kept a man at the bowsprit on watch each night in case the ship should suffer the same fate as had befallen a number of Dutch vessels and be wrecked on the totally uncharted coast. There was no cause for alarm, however, and by the beginning of May the *Griffin* was safely anchored in the Batavia road.

If Captain Dethick hoped that some time on shore would do the men good, he was mistaken. Only two days after arriving the log noted: 'At 7 p.m. put James Murray, seaman, in irons for threatening to kill Mr Parslow, Fifth Mate, and striking Mr Chas. Hudson, Chief Mate. In the middle of the night he got his irons off and run away with the yawl from alongside.' Murray was never seen again and next to his name in the log is written 'Run at Batavia'.

On 21 May the *Delaware* arrived and brought the distressing news that her captain, Thomas Dethick's old friend, Abraham Dominicus, had died. The ship had been ravaged by scurvy and had no carpenter, a vital man, so Dethick let them have his carpenter's mate, Samuel

Gregory. Three days later, the *Griffin* was due to sail and the captain and supracargoes came back on board, having been guests of the Dutch Governor on shore. They were surprised to find that their servants and some other seamen had not arrived, as they had set out the night before. After waiting for some hours Captain Dethick sent a boat to find out what had happened. Soon after they found one of the passenger's servants on shore; the log told his story: 'They were attacked by ten people armed in a Mallay Prow about 11 at night, who cut them all off but him, and he escaped by their imagining him to be dead. They rifled the boat and put a hole in her bottom.' The *Griffin* lost six men including the captain's steward, Edward Beardmore, who had sailed on the 1749–50 voyage. The next day they must have been glad to hoist sail and leave Batavia.

By the end of June they were anchored at Whampoa, having negotiated the islands without incident. The supracargoes and Captain Dethick went up to Canton as usual and the remaining crew unloaded the ship during July, but on the 27th another case of insubordination resulted in a man being put in irons and the captain was recalled.

In early August a strange custom was enacted when one of the Chinese customs officers, described in the log as the 'Grand Mandarin', came on board with his entourage in order to measure the ship. The Chinese regarded the length of the ship as the distance between the mizzen-mast and fore-mast and then took into account the breadth (but not the depth) and, after a complicated calculation, levied port fees accordingly. As stated earlier, this bizarre method produced a figure which no one understood and somehow varied every time a ship was measured. As the records are incomplete, there is only one set of figures for the *Griffin*'s measurement, in 1760, and she was computed at 182.4 units, which attracted a charge of 1,359 taels. To this sum was added a statutory gratuity of 1,950 taels, and the total came to 3,309 taels or £1,103.

August passed with further unloading and September, October and November was taken up with receiving cargo, stowing it away and restocking with provisions. Captain Dethick must have been enthusiastic about both his own and the crew's victuals because, for this voyage, he had created three new positions: those of captain's cook's mate, poulterer and butcher. His belief in the value of good food was well founded and highly successful as, for the *Griffin*'s first two voyages, not one man died as a result of bad provisions, except when the supply was out of the Captain's control, and, furthermore, for the ship's entire life not one man succumbed to scurvy, which only broke out once. Dethick also had a baker and there are several references during October to baking bread on Whampoa Island, which is interesting, as seventeen years later, when William Hickey sailed on the *Plassey*, he noted that bread was not commonly carried on Indiamen and that it was the foodstuff he missed most of all during a long voyage.

On 2 December the *Griffin* weighed anchor and began her trip down the Pearl River. During the next two days she passed over the two bars with no trouble and, on the 9th, the captain and supracargoes came on board and she set sail for home. A week or so later a curious ritual was performed when the captain 'sold all the dead people's things at the mast'. This was done by auction and traditionally the officers and crew would pay considerably more than the value of the goods on offer as a charitable gesture to the family of a dead companion. The purser, at the end of the voyage, would deduct the money from wages and pass it on to the next of kin.

Early in January 1754 the ship made a watering stop for two days at Princess Island, which lies at the southern end of the Straits of Sunda, and then there was no other stop or even sight of land until St Helena was reached two months later. During this time the crew were kept busy with the day-to-day sailing of the ship and later cleaning her for the arrival at St Helena. With so much livestock on board, all of which was kept and fed on deck, the ship became very messy and so it was completely washed down and scrubbed twice a week, but for arrival in port more elaborate measures were taken which often involved painting and tarring. The sailmakers were also busy, as the log reports them darning and repairing the 'best sails, they being pretty much eaten by rats'.

As before the Governor and his lady were entertained on board and then the ship set sail, in company with two others, after a stay of just over two weeks. They did not stop at Ascension, but steered a course directly for home and had first sight of England on 19 May. By early June the *Griffin* was anchored at Gravesend and moved up to Blackwall. On 18 July the customs officers came on board and cleared the ship, which signalled the end of the second voyage.

Somewhat unusually, it was Charles Hudson who took the log book and manifests up to India House on 23 July, but he wrote, 'Captain Dethick being in the country for his health with the leave of the Court, is the reason Mr Hudson the Chief Mate has signed this book and the list of Private Trade.'

The cycle began again a year later, but for the second time the *Griffin*'s tender bore a new name. On this occasion it was Francis Salvador's name that was missing, for he had been taken ill and decided to retire to Bath, then a rapidly developing health spa relying on the heated mineral springs. He had handed over all his affairs to his son Joseph and his name, together with those of Captains Thomas Hunt and Thomas Dethick (now fully recovered), appeared on the document submitted to the Company's Court. The *Griffin* was put into the ballot and duly declared to sail in the 1755 season.

Most of the old officers and crew had already sailed on other ships and one, the *Rhoda* under Captain Macnamara, had enticed the Griffin's old second, third, and fifth mates. Two of them ended their sea days on the *Rhoda*, but John Parslow continued for many years, retiring as chief mate of the *Triton* in 1770 after two long voyages in that position. Thomas Dethick still had his friend Charles Hudson for chief mate and soon appointed William Hoskins, John Clements and Robert Oxlade as second, third and fourth mates. For the fifth mate, he went to his own family and recruited the brother of his sister Elizabeth's husband, William Statham. Thomas Liell, who had been a supracargo on the previous voyage asked if his son Thomas could be found a position, and he was duly appointed midshipman. This marked the beginning of a long and distinguished career in the Company's marine service which culminated in him becoming both captain and husband of the *Stafford* from 1770. Two sailors from the last trip were promoted – Andrew Mitchell to quartermaster and John Read to captain's hoopman – and Dethick kept his two servants, Thomas Godfrey and John Maugham.

Relations between France and England had deteriorated since the end of the second voyage and war, which was already in progress in India, was imminent in Europe, thus, when the *Griffin* came out of dry dock at Blackwall on 22 August 1755, her cargo included seven chests of muskets and bayonets, and a large quantity of grapeshot and gun powder. The Company once again gave China as her destination and decided to divert the *Griffin* from her usual course and named St Helena as the first port of call. The garrison there was under threat of siege, so even more war materials were put on board and forty-one soldiers were added to the ship's company.

The middle of October found the *Griffin* at the Downs together with several men-of-war and merchantmen destined for all over Europe or the Caribbean, and one other East Indiaman. They set sail on 1 November and headed into the Atlantic with HMS *Ipswich* (seventy-four guns) and HMS *Revenge* (sixty-four guns) offering protection.

The other Indiaman, the *Delaware*, was a slow ship compared with the *Griffin* and she found herself, over the next six weeks, once the convoy had dispersed, continually shortening her sails to allow the other ship to catch up. On 19 December they kept a look out for the coast of Brazil and Captain Dethick wrote in the log: 'At 1 p.m. spoke to Captain Winter to get his letters ready against tomorrow and I will take them on board as we are now out of the way of the enemy and lose time in company, I thought it best to part as we may arrive at St Helena as soon as possible.'

The *Griffin* arrived at St Helena on New Year's Day 1756 and disgorged a huge quantity of stores and soldiers. The ship had been so weighed down with extra cannons and shot that without them the captain found that his ballast was insufficient, so an extra forty-three boat loads full of sand had to be brought on board. The stay of seven weeks was much longer than usual, but the ship departed on 20 February and went around the Cape of Good Hope on 18 March.

St Paul was seen a month later and by the end of April the captain was keeping a close watch for shoals off the coast of western Australia and fixed a new course of north-north-east. There was now a possibility of encountering stray ships from the French East Indies fleet so all guns were cleaned out and reloaded in case the powder had become damp and, as the coast of Java came into sight, the crew were kept on round-the-clock lookout.

As it turned out, no other ships were seen and the *Griffin* anchored at Batavia on 15 May. This place must have held bad memories for Dethick and Hudson, but they were forced to take on more water together with rice and arrack, and to embark three new supracargoes, Thomas Fitzhugh, James Flint and Benjamin Torin, who had been waiting there since the previous year.

The reason for this was that the Griffin's destination was not Canton but the rarely visited Chinese city of Ningpo (known to them as Limpo). During the previous century trade had been limited to Canton, but, after the amalgamation of the old and new Companies in 1708, a decision was taken to try to open up more ports. Expeditions were sent up the coast to Amoy and Ningpo (whose anchorage was at Chusan) as it was felt that these places, being nearer to the tea growing areas, would provide more plentiful and cheaper merchandise. The Chinese took a completely different view and purposely kept stocks low and made life as difficult as possible for the English merchants, giving as their reason that the shorter distance meant the tea passed fewer customs posts and cost the Emperor through lost duties. Amoy was given up in 1734 and no ships went to Ningpo from 1736.

In 1754, however, the Company's supracargoes at Canton became infuriated with the attitude and corruption of the Chinese officials and determined to try one ship at Ningpo the following season. The *Earl of Holderness* was duly dispatched with three senior supracargoes on board and a young man named Thomas Bevan, who, like James Flint, had been sent to China in order to learn the language and become an interpreter. Before long his schoolmaster had suddenly been taken away by officials who explained that the Englishman would be able, should he master the language, to send letters directly to Peking without them first being censored in Canton, but his understanding was sufficient to be of great use.

The *Earl of Holderness* found the local Chinese officials at Ningpo keen to do business and they agreed to all the conditions laid down. As the season went on, however, a more senior mandarin became involved and attempted to overturn the agreements already reached. He grew extremely difficult and the supracargoes suspected an involvement with the officials from Canton, who stood to lose a great deal should the Company take its business entirely to Ningpo. A tolerably good cargo was purchased despite the problems, and taxes and gratuities on a lower scale than that at Canton still made the place attractive. In their report the experience was summed up by the supracargoes as follows: 'The whole business of the year was carried on with some difficulty which was reasonable to be expected.'

With her new supracargoes on board, the *Griffin* left Batavia on 2 June and headed for China. Within a week, however, the crew came down with the flux or dysentery, obviously contracted from the water taken on at Batavia and three men died. In the log Dethick wrote, 'Several of our people are taken ill every day'. A crew reduced in strength and number finds it difficult to sail a ship at the best of times, but in the treacherous waters around Sumatra and Borneo the *Griffin* had to be hauled up quickly when she came several times into shoal water. She found the islands near Macau on 1 July and then gingerly felt her way up the coast, travelling through waters none of them knew and about which the pilot books were very vague. On the 12th they anchored at Kittow Point just outside the Chusan anchorage and the supracargoes set off for Ningpo in the pinnace. A few hours later the longboat was sent after them with stores, and the ship was asked to wait until news was received.

Four days later no word had been heard and the *Griffin* was surrounded by Chinese men-of-war junks. Dethick wrote: 'I was suspicious of their having some design on us, so thought it proper to load and prime all the guns and keep the small arms loaded upon the gratings on the Quarterdeck and keep to strict look out, watch and watch all night.' Another four days went by and word came from Mr Fitzhugh saying they were waiting for a chop to allow the ship in. There was no more word and on the 24th Dethick wrote: 'I fear something not right has happened, but as we have eighteen people out of the ship and many ill on board I don't care to weaken the ship any more by sending the yawl to Chusan to know what is the matter and for fear they should detain her.'

The next day, to everyone's great relief, the two ship's boats came back with permission to go in. Dethick and Hudson both went off to sound for a channel and it was not until the 31st that the ship was able to creep in. The next four months passed with unloading, repairing and reloading, and was, as far as the ship's company was concerned, much like life at Canton with the exception that two of the crew including the fifth mate, William Statham, died.

Up at Ningpo things were very different. When the supracargoes first arrived they found that the two *hongists* with whom they had done business the previous year had declared that the Englishmen had left without paying them. The *towya*, who was a local official, had apparently listened to them, but was soon convinced of the spuriousness of their statements and permitted trade to begin. The Englishmen asked for their ship to be allowed up river to Ningpo as the passage of their goods down to Chusan, where the *Griffin* lay, took seven or eight days and during that time were damaged or pilfered. Dethick was asked to survey the river and reported that it was not safely navigable, so the scheme was dropped. The *tsontock* of the province, who last year had been suspected of being in league with his compeer at Canton, was still truculent but, other than insisting on the absolute letter of the law, did not make any further attempt to halt trade.

By the end of January 1757 the cargo was complete and the supra-cargoes came down to the ship. On the 24th they hauled all the cannons back on board (the *tsontock* had ordered they be removed together with the gunpowder and small arms) and reloaded them. After receiving permission to depart, the *Griffin* sailed on the 30th. The next year the *Onslow* came to Ningpo only to find no goods in the *hongs* and the charges doubled. After this no Indiamen went to Ningpo again, so the *Griffin* was the penultimate ship to trade there.

Throughout February, as they sailed towards Batavia in order to disembark the supracargoes, the weather worsened as the *Griffin* had left China about three weeks later than she should have done and the monsoons were beginning to blow the wrong way. On the 23rd they saw two unidentified vessels and, worried about their nationality, Dethick wrote a report in the log:

A consultation aboard the Griffin 23 Febry. 1757. We weighed at daylight and at 8 a.m. in the morning saw two ships standing along shore distance about 3 leagues [9 miles]. In about ½ an hour they hauled up upon a wind and stood towards us on which we tacked and stood from them and made the signal of the year 1755. One of them lowered her fore top gallant sail and hoisted a signal but we could not distinguish what it was. After chasing us about half an hour and rather coming up with us, they bore away and stood in for land again. From the above circumstances we imagined they could not be enemies, but two of His Majesty's ships that (were) afraid of driving us to leeward off the straits. Therefore, we unanimously agreed to tack and stand in again for the Straits of Malacca according to the Honble. Company's orders.

During the next two days the ships were again often in sight and were finally identified as two other Indiamen, the *Harcourt* and *Stormont*, which had been at Canton. Later they all met up at Batavia and dined on each other's ships. There once again the water taken on proved to be contaminated and claimed the lives of two more of the crew, including the second mate, William Hoskins.

The *Griffin* was now sailing with the other Indiamen and, as they approached the Cape of Good Hope, Captain Dethick spoke with the commodore, Captain William Webber of the *Harcourt*. His orders from the Company stated that he should keep in company with other Indiamen should he meet them, but at the same time sail at least 100 leagues to the South of the Cape. Captain Webber, who had the same orders, said he preferred to see how the winds took them. As this might later prove to be a questionable point, Dethick decided to record his actions in the log and wrote:

When our boat returned, I sent for my Officers (who now only numbered three, two having died) and told them of what orders I had and showed them my letter to Capt. Webber, with his answer and they unanimously advised me to comply with my last orders and, if possible, to keep company with the two ships, which entirely agrees with my own opinion as there is probably a war, and the season is so late that we may lose the opportunity of a convoy from St Helena should we be obliged to beat long off the Cape.

On 27 June St Helena was reached safely and they found three other Indiamen and a man-of-war, HMS *Colchester* anchored there. They left together on 10 August and headed for Ascension, where the season for turtles was over and the seamen came away empty handed. The small squadron formed a line of battle abreast in order hopefully to deceive any French ships and on 1 November fell in with Commodore Keppell and four ships of the Royal Navy. This was a considerable comfort, but the problem was that most of the *Griffin*'s crew were then impressed into the King's ships, which had suffered casualties on the North American station. The ship could not function at all, so some were returned and a few days later the English coast was sighted. They anchored at Spithead and fifty-two men were taken off to HMS *Pembroke*, leaving only forty-one aboard.

During the next two weeks the anchorage filled up with other merchantmen and men-of-war. On 28 November the patrols reported no French activity in the Channel and the *Nassau* sent the *Griffin* forty men so she could be sailed, and she, together with 'about sixty or seventy sail of other merchantmen' and a number of naval vessels sailed around to Margate. It must have presented a magnificent spectacle for anyone on land.

By December the *Griffin* was safely back at Gravesend and being unloaded. For no apparent reason, the process took longer than before and it was not until 6 February 1758 that the arrival of the customs officials signified that her third voyage had come to a successful conclusion.

Preparations for the fourth voyage began later that same year with the acceptance of the *Griffin*'s tender in October. The war, which had been expected to begin as the *Griffin* departed in 1755, had in fact done so whilst the ship was sailing back from China. After initial reverses, the English were defeating the French in Europe, Canada and the West Indies and had most of her ports blockaded. The campaign in India had been conducted brilliantly by Robert Clive and culminated in his victory over the French-backed Nawab of Bengal at Plassey in 1757, and the Company now occupied almost all the French forts.

The Directors summed up the situation perfectly when they wrote to the factors at Fort William in November 1758 saying, 'The war with France is still continued with great vigour and we have the pleasure of saying that, by the steady conduct of our Government and the superior force and success of the British Navy, that of France is greatly reduced and the remainder confined in a great measure to their ports.' This letter also advised the names of the twenty-one ships stationed for 1758, where the *Griffin* is listed as due to sail to Bombay. They went on to remark, 'The China trade has been gradually improving and in consequence become one of the principle objects of the Company's attention.' In fact, the profits from tea were paying for Clive's conquests.

Most of the old crew had dispersed, many of them probably being caught by the press gang as they drank their wages away in the music houses and gambling dens along the banks of the River Thames at Rotherhithe and Wapping. Much has been written about the brutality and indiscriminate nature of the press gang but, in fact, few landsmen were taken because, in all ports, sailors on leave or resting were immediately recognizable by their appearance, 'dialect and manner peculiar to themselves'. The hard outdoor life left even young men prematurely aged, while disfigured hands and tattoos (often applied with gunpowder) were instant give-aways. Their manner of dress was also unique and the average sailor tended to wear a pair of very wide, baggy breeches often striped or tarred and cut several inches below the knee. Many of them wore checked shirts or a blue fearnought jacket and Monmouth cap.

During the 1750s there were upwards of 60,000 experienced mariners in England and their numbers grew every day as men volunteered, often as a result of economic necessity, so, even if there was a war on, the Company never had any difficulty in attracting crewmen. Thomas Dethick, as usual, looked around for officers and recruited David Saunders from the *Walpole* as second mate, James Swithin from *Lord Anson* became third mate and Fryer Todd, who had been wrecked on his previous voyage in the *York*, was made fourth mate.

Dethick did not subscribe to the usual policy of employing young potential officers in the role of captain's servant, possibly because he was never one himself, but over the years a number of young gentlemen had gone in his ships as ordinary seamen. For the third voyage, Henry Littleton had been in such a position, but had obviously proved himself as he was now appointed fifth mate. The surgeon was the most experienced man sailing at that time in this rank : John McFarquhar had begun his sea service fifteen years earlier in 1744 and, up to his appointment on the *Griffin*, had sailed in five other Indiamen. The purser's place was filled by Samuel Statham, brother of William who had died on the previous voyage and Thomas Dethick's brother-in-law. Being a purser was an enviable position as they were given a generous private trade allowance and were also able to stock up with various luxuries and drink which could be sold to the seamen during the voyage, although not at a profit exceeding 50%. Many commanders put their sons or friends into such an office and even surgeons, who were also permitted a large private trade, did well. The most famous was Robert Wigram, who rose from being surgeon on the *Duke of Richmond* in 1764 to be one of the largest owners ever of Indiamen by 1810.

From the previous voyage a far higher proportion of petty officers than previously signed on again, including the gunner, John Wyllie, cooper Charles Butcher and carpenter Thomas Cock together with his mate, John Wood. John Read and Thomas Godfrey, both of whom had made two previous trips on the *Griffin*, were also to be found among the ship's company as ship's steward and captain's servant respectively. It seems that supracargo Thomas Liell was pleased with the progress his eldest son made on the *Griffin*'s last trip, as he entered another son, Richard, as a seaman, and several other gentlemen also sailed below decks including John Barfoot, Thomas Eaden and Andrew Todd, brother of the fourth mate.

The Company told its Indian factors that for the 1759 ships 'a considerable part of the tonnage will be taken up in the passage of military recruits and the extraordinary quantity of military and other stores indented for', and the *Griffin*'s manifest certainly echoes this: 58 soldiers, 10,000 iron shot, 2,000 iron shells, 24 chests of small arms, 30 long shells and 450 'double headed shot', amongst other things. Even the captain became involved, as his private trade included 2 chests of trading guns and one chest of flints. It is the items for the English settlers in India, however, which form the most interesting part of the private trade cargo as their requirements were to be satisfied with such things as 2 cases of spectacles, 3 boxes of hats, 5 of stationery, 2 cases of tablecloths, 3 cases of 'apparel' and 1 box each of toys, table clocks, looking-glasses and ink.

Loading continued for six weeks and on 13 March 1759 the *Griffin* sailed for Spithead, where she found about fifty other merchant ships, three East Indiamen and several men-of-war. On the 27th, her passengers, Mrs Drake, Major Frazer, Mr Morley and Mr Poyton, the commander of the troops, came on board and the next day a great fleet set sail with HMS *Norwich* and *Echo* on patrol as far as the Bay of Biscay.

These vessels parted on 7 May and 'we gave [them] three cheers' before continuing on in company with the *Harcourt*, *Godolphin* and *Clinton*. The voyage was unmemorable, although during June the third mate, James Swithin, had reason for complaint when one of the midshipmen, William Corboyd, refused to obey an order and 'Dam'd his blood and asked him who he was' whilst 'forcing his fist almost in his face'. Mr Swithin reported that he pushed the man away, upon which Corboyd 'struck him and continued his blows until he was prevented by Thompson the Quartermaster'. Corboyd was tried and the matter was 'plainly proved to be done to an officer on Duty in so Public a manner'. He was tied to the mast and received a dozen lashes.

At the end of August, after five months without sight of land, the *Griffin*, unusually, decided to make a stop at Madagascar for food and water. They stayed eight days, during which time two seamen were drowned after their boat capsized and a visit was made to the King of Marandava.

On 3 October Malabar Point was sighted and later in the day the ship entered Bombay harbour. From here, for the next six-and-a-half months, the *Griffin* sailed around India, going down the west coast to settlements such as Goa, Tellicherry and Anjengo, right at the southern tip, and then back up to Surat, before returning to Bombay and Tellicherry. All this time they were continually on the look out for French ships, but spotted none. They lost fourteen men to the flagship of Admiral Pocock, HMS *Yarmouth*, and several men died, but on the whole it was an ordinary voyage which many commanders must have regarded as inordinately dull. The Company had told its servants in India, 'If therefore, you . . . should have ships in your hands at any time which for want for goods cannot be dispatched home, such ship or ships must be consigned to our Supracargoes at Canton . . . .'

The *Griffin* was obviously considered surplus to Indian requirements because, on 26 April 1759, she sailed for China. Once again a stop was made at Batavia, where the *Oxford* under Captain Webber was riding. On 28 June the captain 'sent the boats again [for water], but being attacked by four Mallay Prows, and one of Captain Webber's people killed, they returned'. Subsequently, Captain Dethick, 'finding the people would hazard their lives going again on shore', hauled up the anchor and sailed away from Batavia, a place which caused him nothing but trouble over the years. They arrived at Whampoa on 15 July and found two other English East Indiamen, *Valentine* and *Suffolk*, and a Swedish ship already there. Shortly afterwards *Pocock* and *Oxford* arrived, so there were five captains staying at the English building in Canton.

Earlier in 1759 one of the Company's ships, the *Pitt*, reached Canton, having made her way from India at a time when everyone considered the winds made a passage impossible. The *Pitt* had arrived late in the season and her captain decided to sail east along the coast of Java and past Celebes before passing through a stretch of water which they named Pitt Strait to the coast of New Guinea. They now found themselves in the Pacific Ocean, so headed north and passed the islands of Mindanao and Luzon before striking out for Formosa and, finally, the coast of China.

The captain of the *Pitt*, William Wilson, was an experienced commander who had realized, whilst landing troops at Fort St George, Madras, that she might not be able to make Canton. It is reasonable to assume that the *Pitt*'s subsequent voyage was not taken on a whim and that he probably spoke to the fort's governor, George Pigot, of his scheme. Pigot was interested in the idea of expanding British interests throughout the Spice Islands, but had been frustrated in his previous endeavours by the Dutch, who kept details of the safe passages for sailing a closely guarded secret. He was advised by a young Company writer, Alexander Dalrymple, who had made a detailed study of the historical papers kept at Fort St George, and he was influenced by the travels of a Company sponsored explorer, Alexander Roid. In 1715 Roid travelled extensively throughout Madagascar, Sumatra, Borneo and Java, and wrote that he had been 'conversant with the barbarous natives on each [of the places he visited] but the greatest barbarians are the Dutch'. More important were his observations from northern Borneo, where he wrote:

It is no wonder that pepper should be dearer this than former years, for when Your Honours had a settlement at Banjan no more than two or three junks at most came yearly, whereas this year there are seven large ones ... This place is as commodiously situated for the English trade as Batavia is for the Dutch.

Dalrymple probably suggested that the commanders of earlier Indiamen had investigated all sorts of possible passages and had found that, by sailing up the eastern side of the Philippine Islands, they could reach Japan at any time. Wilson was given permission to use his discretion in attempting the passage and was given a small two-masted vessel, which had been captured from the French named *Success* to go in front and sound for him.

Pigot and Dalrymple were jubilant when they learned of the *Pitt*'s success in a letter from Canton dated 8 May 1759, which read, 'Commodore Wilson who arrived the 4th of last month having made a long and infrequented passage which may in future prove of service to the Hon. Company as no ship need now lose her passage.' Having discovered that an Indiaman could sail to Canton at any time of year, they had decided to try to open up a new centre for British trade and had discovered that the Sulu Islands were a semi-independent group not affected by the Spanish in Manila nor by the Dutch to the south. A plot was hatched to sign an agreement with the ruler of Sulu and, to facilitate its implementation, the scheme was passed on to the secret committee under the guise of exploring the possibilities opened up by the *Pitt*'s voyage. This deception was necessary for their success because an expedition mounted under the auspices of any other body would require the approval of the Court in London and to wait for that could take two years, by which time Pigot could be either retired or dead, such were the uncertainties of life in India. Governor Pigot had at his disposal another captured French vessel named *Cuddalore*, which was commanded by Captain George Best, and the secret committee allowed him to use it for an expedition in the interest of protecting the Company's China ships. Dalrymple set off in the *Winchelsea*, commanded by Thomas Howe (who had been on the *Griffin* as third mate for the second voyage in 1752–54), bound for Malacca, and soon afterwards the *Cuddalore* set out 'to attempt to discover a new route to China through the Molucca Islands and New Guinea, that the China ships may avoid the danger in time of war of going through the Straits of Malacca'.

Dalrymple was waiting at Batavia and took command of the *Cuddalore* with Captain Best in charge of navigation, and they sailed to Macau, arriving on 3 July 1759. On the 6th Dalrymple wrote to the supracargoes at Canton declaring that he had been headed for Manila (which was untrue), but had been forced into Macau when the ship ran short of provisions. As it was impossible for a ship to come into Whampoa without paying the measurage fee and gratuity, the supracargoes suggested he wait for an Indiaman's arrival and then come into Canton on board that, leaving the *Cuddalore* at Macau. Later in the month the Chinese had become very suspicious of the *Cuddalore*'s reason for remaining outside Whampoa and insisted on measuring her anyway. Dalrymple wrote to say that he was considering putting out to sea and received a reply saying he could do whatever he liked. At the same time two French ships were said to be cruising along the coast, so Dalrymple suggested he would go to look for them.

The French ships came into Whampoa, which was a neutral port, and nothing more was heard of the *Cuddalore* until 18 October, when a letter was received from Dalrymple in Macau, saying he had come in there 'after being disappointed in his attempt to return to Madras'. Whether he did this or went instead to the northern Philippines, as is stated in some texts, is unclear and this three-month period remains a mystery. What is certain, however, is that Dalrymple adopted a high-handed attitude with the Portuguese authorities over a number of seamen who had run from the ship and for some months did nothing constructive whatsoever, presumably being at a loss to know what to do.

By June he appears to have completed a voyage along the coast of China and probably spoke to the *Griffin* when she arrived off Macau on the 13th. Four days later the Chinese were perplexed when, upon examining the ship, they found more guns than had been on board a few months earlier. Dalrymple would only comment, 'The folly of these people is past comprehension, they even took a copper pump for a gun and were not to be persuaded what it was until we showed them the use of it', before sailing off again and making interesting observations on the island of Hainan, which he later explained in a letter to William Pitt, the English Prime Minister.

The *Cuddalore* returned to Macau in September and Dalrymple proceeded to put his master plan into action, suggesting to the supracargoes at Canton that he remain there until the Indiamen were ready to go home. Intelligence had already been received of the presence of a strong French force in the Straits of Sunda, which was the route the ships would usually use. It seems that Dalrymple had genuinely intended to explore the eastern coast of the Philippines and go from there to Mindanao before turning west and ending up in the Sulu archipelago, but the combination of his attitude towards the Chinese and Portuguese officials and French expansion into Sumatra had prevented this. The idea of escorting the ships back to India was a brilliant one as it satisfied all parties and even demonstrated to the secret committee that he was doing what they thought he was.

The five Indiamen, *Griffin*, *Valentine*, *Pocock*, *Oxford* and *Suffolk*, were all ready to depart by the end of December and on the 23rd the supracargoes wrote to Dalrymple, who had been allowed to bring the *Cuddalore* into Whampoa when he revealed that she was in need of repair, requesting him 'to accompany the ships through the China seas, to which he most readily promised us'.

All the ships left Whampoa at 9 a.m. on 31 December and the voyage officially began once they passed the Ladrone Islands, which they did on 1 January 1761. Exactly three weeks later the *Griffin* sank.

CHAPTER 5

Search for the Griffin

For students of both maritime history and naval architecture the East Indiamen are a fascinating study. It was these ships which, in addition to being the mainstay of the Company's trade, provided transport for those who conquered India, opened China to the West and made the earliest accurate charts of the Far East and Pacific. They were also the precursors of the famous tea clippers, of which one, the *Cutty Sark*, remains preserved in the River Thames to give her visitors an idea of how the ships worked and of the conditions in which the sailors lived during the early nineteenth century. Of their eighteenth-century predecessors, none survive, even as replicas and the only relics we have of the ships which founded an empire are a few paintings, most of which are held in gallery stores, a model on show at the National Maritime Museum and several plans. There is not even a museum to the memory of the East India Company.

Some English East Indiamen have been salvaged, but to date little of interest has been recovered due to the ships in question being dashed on rocks and broken up. Even though the English Company lost over 100 ships in the century up to 1800, only five of these were on return voyage from China and these have always presented the greatest interest for the non-institutional archaeologist as the possibility of recouping some of the enormous cost of salvage is present. These China ships are of interest not only for their construction and the artefacts associated with those who manned them, but also because the cargoes of porcelain and other Chinese products can assist historians and collectors in dating existing pieces. Of these five Indiamen, one simply disappeared, one was wrecked on the English coast and plundered, another went down near Madagascar and was looted, and the remaining two were lost in the Philippines.

In 1984 the National Museum of the Philippines approached French archaeologist Franck Goddio with an offer to grant a permit for exploration and possible excavation of a coral reef off Palawan called the Royal Captain Shoal. It was named after one of the two East India

Company ships to sink after being in Canton, the *Royal Captain*, which was lost in 1773. Research for this project took nearly a year to complete and, during the course of this, any information on the other China ship, the *Griffin,* was noted and recorded. An official permit was issued to Franck for the Royal Captain Shoal on 28 March 1985 and, at the same time, he asked for and was granted another to cover the rough area in which the *Griffin* was believed to have sunk. The area which this permit covered was a large one as much more work would need to be done before any definite search commenced, and extended from 6°0'N to 7°0'N and 121°0' to 122°0'. The permit was valid for two years and Franck's intention was to look for the *Griffin* once the *Royal Captain* had been located. The study of changes in the nature of porcelain cargoes and designs over the thirteen years which spanned the two wrecks would have been fascinating for Chinese historians and, as the *Griffin* represented the last of the old type of 499-ton Indiamen and the *Royal Captain* was built in a transition period which led to the introduction of 1,200-ton ships, the differences in construction would shed much light in a hitherto unknown field.

Franck enlisted the help of an Australian expatriate, Kim Barnaby, who had lived in the Philippines for many years and was an experienced diver who ran a company called Promar, specializing in providing logistical help and personnel for ventures of this nature. They then went off to find the *Royal Captain*.

During this time Kris Shaffer was on board the 115-foot schooner *Sol*. She is a magnificent vessel, built in 1973 and previously used to supply the inhabitants of Lord Howe Island, about 350 miles off the east coast of Australia. In 1976 she was purchased by a film company and, after undergoing full restoration, was put to work. Kris was on board for several years and his 1985 project was later released under the title *Slave Ships of the Sulu Sea*. It is the story of an extraordinary group of fishermen called the Muro Ami, who for ten months each year continuously ply the waters of the southern Philippines in battered old ships. These are literally teeming with young children who dive down to the reef holding strings with plastic strips and metal balls attached in order to disorientate the fish and indiscriminately herd every species into their vast nets. They return to each site regularly and eventually their methods leave the reefs completely barren and the ecological system breaks down for years.

For as long as he can remember Kris has been fascinated by the sea and everything concerning the marine environment. He has produced documentaries on a wide range of maritime subjects and, always curious about shipwrecks, had previously made a film on the sunken Japanese warships in Truk Lagoon.

At the end of 1985 Kris was in Manila and at the Yacht Club was introduced to Kim Barnaby, a well-known figure there. Learning of his interest, Kim told Kris about the Royal Captain Shoal project. Meanwhile, Franck had failed to find the *Royal Captain*'s wreck, but had instead found the remains of a sixteenth-century Chinese trading ship, which he was excavating. Kim also mentioned the *Griffin* and this immediately roused Kris's interest as, during the shooting of the Muro Ami film, *Sol* had often sailed past a reef in the Sulu Sea called Griffin Rocks. 'That must be where she sank,' said Kim.

Not long afterwards Franck arrived in Manila and was introduced to Kris. On the whole the Royal Captain Shoal had been disappointing: the only artefacts which could have possibly belonged to an East Indiamen being a small four-pounder cannon and a large eighteenth-century anchor. These could have come from a number of other ships, but Franck felt certain that they were from the *Royal Captain*. The reef falls away very quickly and he believes that the ship sank in deep water and will never be found. Franck had already used Kim's boat the *Sea Wind* and considered her unsuitable for a long excavation on the *Griffin* site, so he was interested to learn of the *Sol*. She was, however, shortly to go into the yard for a major overhaul which would include the fitting of an interior steel skin to cope with a proposed filming voyage to the Antarctic. Kris then introduced Franck to Terry Restall, who captained a 112-foot former oil-rig tender vessel called *Load Star*. With a few minor alterations she would be perfect for the expedition, and Kris and Terry decided to postpone all their other plans and accept Franck's offer of a partnership to develop the *Griffin* project.

Franck's information on the ship was only fragmentary, as his research had obviously concentrated on the *Royal Captain*. Confirmation of the *Griffin*'s wreck was found in the 'bible' of East Indiamen records, Hardy's *Register of East India Company Ships*, which simply said: '1761, *Griffin* 499 tons: Lost.' The information which had led Franck to apply for his permit in the area of Sulu Island was found in another book which said 'lost at the island of Zelo' (*sic*). The experience on the Royal Captain Shoal had taught everyone that research is the key to looking for shipwrecks. Franck had obtained most of his information on the *Royal Captain* from the log of the ship, which had been saved, but we hoped that a more detailed investigation into the *Griffin* would produce more and, hopefully, some first-hand accounts. This was of the greatest importance because with the failure to find the *Royal Captain,* the *Griffin* now looked like the only English China ship which would ever be found – assuming we could turn up enough evidence to make a search worthwhile.

Several months later the search was transferred to London, to the reading room of the British Library. The first step was to check if Lloyd's List, which publishes details of all ship movements, existed at that time – which it did. We did not know exactly when in 1761 the *Griffin* was lost or, indeed, if the date was even correct, so to begin with the entire year's issues of Lloyd's List were requested on microfilm. Looking through this is a slow job and the first six months of these were read without finding anything remotely of interest. On the second day of searching, however, in an issue dated 1 September 1761, we found it. The entry said: 'The *Griffin,* Dethick, from China for London, is lost in the Streights of Java, but the crew is saved.' This was a great disappointment, as the Straits of Java, which presumably meant the Malacca Strait, begin over 1,400 miles from Griffin Rocks. We knew that Indiamen did not usually sail through the Philippines but set a course direct from Canton to either the Malacca or Sunda Straits, so this information was not wholly unexpected, but we thought, having come this far, it was still worth following up, just to make absolutely sure.

Our next call was to the wonderful collection of documents pertaining to the East India Company which is housed in a separate part of the British Library called the India Office Library and Records. When the Company was dissolved in 1858, a new Government department, the India Office, was created and all the old archives were passed to this body. The India Office was responsible for governing India until independence came in 1947 and after that date the collection, by then considerably larger, was transferred to the Commonwealth Relations Office. In 1967 the library moved from the premises in Whitehall which it had occupied for a century to a new building in Blackfriars Road, where it is today. Still expanding with the continual addition of manuscripts and new books, responsibility for the collection's preservation was taken over by the British Library in 1982 and it now contains over 300,000 items, which take up a staggering nine linear miles of shelf space.

In the catalogue hall, besides lists of original documents, are a number of books of general reference, entries of births, deaths and marriages in India before independence and printed copies of the Company's letter books. These contain all the correspondence which passed between various presidencies and factories in India and the Court of Directors in London. Although the series is by no means

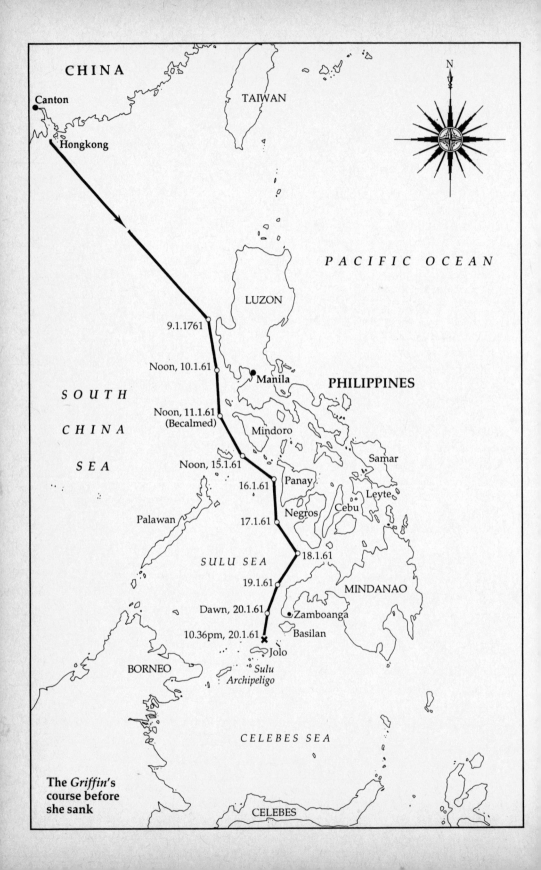

CHINA

Canton

Hongkong

TAIWAN

PACIFIC OCEAN

N

LUZON

9.1.1761

Noon, 10.1.61

Manila

PHILIPPINES

SOUTH

CHINA

SEA

Noon, 11.1.61
(Becalmed)

Mindoro

Noon, 15.1.61

Samar

16.1.61

Panay

Leyte

Palawan

Negros

Cebu

17.1.61

SULU SEA

18.1.61

19.1.61

MINDANAO

Dawn, 20.1.61

Zamboanga

10.36pm, 20.1.61

Basilan

Jolo

BORNEO

Sulu
Archipeligo

CELEBES SEA

The *Griffin's*
course before
she sank

CELEBES

complete, these are the best source for research into what was happening in India and it was to the Fort William (Calcutta)-India House correspondence book for 1760–62 that we turned. In a letter dated 30 September 1761 the *Griffin*'s loss was explained in more detail:

But we have ... been informed by the *Count Moltke* a Danish Ship from Copenhagen that the *Suffolk* imported at St Helena the 27th May from China which brought the disagreeable account that on the 20th January about eleven at night the *Griffin* struck on a rock between Mindinao and Jolo in the Latitude of 6°48' North and was unfortunately lost. All the people were saved but no part of the cargo as the ship sunk very soon.

A quick glance at the chart confirmed that there could be no doubt that our Griffin Rocks were the same as the ones mentioned in this account. What was even better was that the letter had mentioned the *Suffolk,* which must have witnessed the wreck, and then went on to name three more, *Valentine, Pocock* and *Oxford,* which opened up the possibility of discovering letters or reports on the wreck and that the logs of these ships might shed more light on the actual position and final moments of the *Griffin.* As all of the *Griffin*'s crew had been saved, there was also a chance that her log had survived and that the original transcripts of the inevitable court of inquiry would exist. The next step was to consult the index of original marine records and once again we were in luck: under reference L/Mar/B/603D was the *Griffin*'s log for 1759–60. Obviously Captain Dethick had taken this off the doomed vessel with him, so it was ordered up from the repositories and, while we waited, Hardy's was consulted to see if the other ships had sailed to China at the same time, which they indeed had, so their log-books were also requested.

About thirty minutes later the volume arrived. It was covered in stained yellowed vellum and, when we gingerly opened it, the first page proclaimed in beautiful copperplate handwriting: 'A journal in the ship *Griffin,* Captain Thos. Dethick from England towards Bombay and China in the year 1759'. Under this was further inscribed, in another hand, 'This is my original journal, Thomas Dethick'. Here was a real piece of history, the story of a voyage of adventure undertaken only two years after Clive had won the Battle of Plassey, before Australia was discovered, and when the American colonies still belonged to Britain. There was an extraordinary feeling of exhilaration tinged with sadness as one looked through the pages, reading the optimistic comments about the weather as the ship headed for China. It was like reading a great tragedy whilst already knowing that the heroine dies on the final page.

The last page, of course, confirmed that the ship had struck on a rock and gave the position relative to various landmarks. During the next few days the logs of all the other ships in the convoy were consulted and their movements during the twelve hours before the *Griffin* struck were carefully transcribed. This was not nearly as easy as it sounds because the eighteenth-century writing and abbreviations had first to be deciphered, and then each island had to be identified by its modern name. We found one called the Hare's Ears and another simply described as a low flat island and so turned to Horsburgh's *India Directory*, which was published for the captains of East Indiamen before Admiralty pilot books existed. This identified the Hare's Ears as Sangboy Islands with two hills of 843 and 626 feet, which could be seen for many miles. The low flat island we knew from sailing in the area described Kaludud, $2\frac{3}{4}$ miles from Griffin Rock, but the *Suffolk* first mentioned it before this island could possibly be in view. This turned out to be St Cruz Island, near Mindanao. This and Kaludud were confirmed in the 1978 Philippine Islands Pilot, but it was slightly mystifying why many of the other islands in the area were not mentioned. Judging from his meticulous entries in previous log-books, we could only imagine that Dethick had made detailed notes in another book which has not survived.

Now that we had the islands and compass point observations, these were transferred on to tracing paper with lines corresponding to the compass fixings radiating from a central point, which represented the ship. A typical entry transcribed in this way was for that of the *Pocock,* which noted: 'At sunset the island Bassolan bore SE, a low flat island SbE$\frac{1}{2}$E and the Hares Ears SSW$\frac{1}{2}$W distance about 4 or 5 leagues and the extremities of Mindana [Mindanao] from NE$\frac{1}{2}$N to EbS$\frac{1}{2}$S.' For each of the five ships there were three or four pieces of tracing paper, each representing a different sighting, which could be moved around on a map until the compass lines and distances corresponded with the landmarks they represented. In this way we finally ended up with five courses drawn on the chart.

We found a number of discrepancies in positions and two ships especially showed considerable inaccuracies, which had to be put down to wrong estimates of distance made in the half-light after sunset, and possible errors in transcription of details by the captain's clerks who wrote the logs, but in the end all the ships were headed in the right direction and spread out over several miles from the *Griffin* in the lead.

Reading through the journals produced a number of references to a schooner or 'snow' called the *Cuddalore* (even though the rigging of the two differs) and also her captain, Alexander Dalrymple. This raised such questions as, what was a schooner doing with a fleet of Indiamen, who was Dalrymple and why were they sailing through unchartered waters, hundreds of miles away from the usual route? We found the answer in a book by Howard Fry entitled *Alexander Dalrymple and the Expansion of British Trade*.

Dalrymple turned out to be an interesting historical personality who, as a fifteen-year-old, arrived in Madras to become a writer in the Company's establishment there. Four years later, in 1757, he had risen to be deputy secretary and was able to study the records of early voyages, a subject which absorbed him. This was the same year in which the Chinese limited foreign trade to Canton only and the Company began looking into the possibility of expanding its operations into Burma, Thailand, Laos, Cambodia and Cochin-China (Vietnam). There was also considerable concern over the decline in the spice business in the wake of a Dutch decision to destroy all spice trees not in their control. The Company still had a factory at Bencoolen in Sumatra, but this was not overly prosperous and it would be desirable to gain a footing elsewhere.

With access to all the documents and intelligence reports, Dalrymple was able to study the situation and its possibilities in great detail, and began to formulate a scheme to enter into a trading treaty with the Sultan of Sulu. He thought that a treaty with this potentate would enable the Company to trade with the Chinese junks which sailed those waters and also find new sources for spice.

His plans were delayed by the French siege of Madras, but, once it was lifted, Dalrymple persuaded the governor, George Pigot, to give him command of the *Cuddalore* and the expedition would be justified as investigating the viability of sailing through the Sulu Sea. In 1759, rather than go to Calcutta where he risked the chance of the *Cuddalore* being requisitioned, Dalrymple sailed to Macau for provisions, Madras having nothing spare because of the siege. He used this as a base for the next eighteen months until the Chinese threatened dire consequences if the ship did not either sail or pay measurage fees.

Dalrymple had found, during his time in Chinese waters, that he had a talent for cartography so he spent most of the time he was sailing to Sulu drawing charts of the islands they passed. When the *Griffin* sank, none of the ships made any mention of the *Cuddalore*'s whereabouts, but a chart Dalrymple drew ten years later showed the ship to be on the blind side of Kaludud, so he had totally failed to guide the Indiamen properly.

Two days after the *Griffin* sank the ships arrived at Sulu and Dalrymple spent the next five days successfully negotiating a treaty of friendship and commerce with the Sultan. They then left and were guided through the Macassar Strait and on to safe waters. The *Cuddalore* surveyed all the islands back towards Sulu and called in there to ratify the treaty, before continuing up to Manila, where Dalrymple received a wary reception. By the end of the year the amount of time he could legitimately justify for the voyage was drawing to a close so he surveyed the western coast of Palawan before arriving back in Madras on 28 January 1762, after an absence of nearly three years. He was not yet twenty-four years old.

The Sulu adventure was ultimately a failure and Dalrymple returned to England in July 1765 determined to write about the search for the great southern continent and propose himself to lead an expedition to find it. He became well known in appropriate circles, but all attempts to obtain a commission from the Royal Navy, who could have provided a vessel, were unsuccessful. In the next few years, however, the Royal Society proposed a voyage to the Pacific in order to observe a transit of Venus which was due on 3 June 1769. The Society obtained the necessary finance and put forward Dalrymple as their choice to lead the expedition. Dalrymple made his position quite clear in that he was only prepared to go as sole commander of the ship and stated he also proposed to search for the southern continent. With this attitude he found himself in dispute with the Admiralty, who insisted that one of their officers captain their ship. Dalrymple, offered a subordinate position, absolutely refused even to go along if he was not totally in charge, so James Cook went instead and discovered the east coast of Australia.

In the 1770s Dalrymple, who by then was a master researcher, occupied himself with several publications and a number of schemes including the study of all available material and accounts concerning attempts to find the North-West Passage. He was sent to Madras as a member of the council in 1775, but returned the following year and set about establishing a reputation as a cartographer, being appointed first official hydrographer to the Company in 1779 and to the Royal Navy in 1795. The next twenty-five years were devoted to publishing charts, promoting surveying expeditions and attempting to ensure that captains of Indiamen were aware of all dangers which could be encountered on their voyages. In old age he became argumentative and the Navy actual dismissed him. He died in 1808.

The Dalrymple involvement added an extra element of interest to the *Griffin*'s story and we called in to see Andrew Cook, who is curator of the map department at the India Office Library and Records. He is an authority on Dalrymple and not only provided us with a number of interesting stories about this extraordinary character but also quickly produced one of his charts drawn in 1771 which actually marked a position with the words '*Griffin* Lost 1761'. A copy of this chart was obtained and, because of its large scale, our pieces of tracing paper made even more sense. Dalrymple's interest in providing Indiamen with all possible information on hazards is attributed by Howard Fry to the loss of the *Earl Talbot* on a well-known reef, a disaster in which his nephew perished, but we like to speculate that it may also have been partially due to his feeling of responsibility for the *Griffin*'s loss, the only wreck in which he was directly involved and one which would not have happened had he been properly discharging his duty.

Attention was now turned to the cargo that was actually on board the *Griffin*. Her log-book catalogues everything which was loaded on board from the first arrival on 9 October to the final shipment from Canton on 22 December 1760, and diligently notes everything belonging to the Company, but is somewhat vague about what formed the officers' private trade. We knew that officers tended to buy more porcelain and other Chinese produce than tea, and two possibilities arose for finding out more about what the log described most often as 'x chests private trade'. The first was to try and find in either county record offices or private collections the personal papers of the officers. This would obviously be a very long job and it was deferred until the second option, that of checking the books kept by the supracargoes in Canton, was followed up. These fall into two categories, the China Factory Diaries and the China Letter Books, which are simply a record of all correspondence to and from Canton, London and Indian presidencies. The factory diaries are altogether much more interesting as they contain not only detailed records of the business done with *hongists*, noting prices, quantities and dispatch dates for all purchases and sales, but also record petitions sent to and received from the authorities, notes concerning the ships at Whampoa and the supracargoes' general feelings about prevailing conditions in Canton. Unfortunately, the series of these books is incomplete during the years 1742 to 1774, but they do exist for 1759–60 as well as for several other years, so the *Griffin*'s cargo was able to be cross-referenced between what was dispatched from Canton and received on board. We could follow the goods from the date they were ordered to delivery and through the process of packing and tarring the chests right up to the time they were stowed away in the hold.

The date shipments from Canton were dispatched down to Whampoa matched exactly with the ship's log noting arrivals, so the official manifest was complete. By its very nature, the private trade was not the concern of the supracargoes, so this information did not appear in any detail in the diary, but we could piece together what small entries there were with the notes in the log, and ended up with an intelligent estimation of what the officers purchased. This was based on comparing the dates that certain goods were dispatched from Canton, for example chinaware, with notes of private trade arrivals on board and, as we knew that porcelain was loaded first, if the Company sent ninety chests to the *Griffin* on 9 October and the officers sent ninety-nine chests on the same or a couple of days later, it stood to reason that these also contained chinaware.

We prepared a final cargo list which looked like this:

CHESTS

	Whole	Half	Quarter	Pecul
Chinaware	6	84		
Chinaware private trade	99			
'Belonging to Mr Wood'* (probably chinaware)	5			
'Some Chinaware private trade'	?			
Tea: Bohea	900	100		
Twankay (a type of Singlo)	510			
Singlo	527		941†	200
Hyson	675			
Hyson Private Trade	120			
Souchon (or Congo)	114			
Nanking Cloth (Nankeens)	20	bundles totalling 800 pieces		

There are a further 5 entries for private trade. The quantity and contents of this is unknown.

* Francis Wood was a supracargo based in Canton.
† Includes 100 'small chests'.

We now knew what was on board the *Griffin* and, as only the chinaware would have survived underwater for over 200 years, it was vitally important to make an estimate, based on the number of pieces per chest, of the quantity on board. There were occasional references to the weight of a chest of tea, which varied between 360 lbs and 67 lbs. (In 1760 Bohea tea, the cheapest, was packed in 360-lb chests. The more expensive types were in 84- and 67-lb chests.) However, as the chinaware was used as extra ballast, these chests were presumably heavier. All the existing factory diary books and letter books between 1741 and 1760 were checked and only four entries were found, relating to twelve separate purchases of varying numbers of chests with no mention whatsoever of their dimensions, so the idea of constructing a chest and filling it with modern china was scrapped. Instead we worked out how much the supracargoes had paid for the *Griffin*'s chinaware, which came to approximately 32 taels for a whole chest and 16 for a half chest, and then checked the prices and contents of the four entries we had found.

In 1759 the supracargoes had purchased 50 chests for a price of 32 taels each, containing a total of nearly 40,000 pieces or 800 per chest. We felt quite sure that this was partially for the *Griffin* as the chinaware would have been ordered in advance and the figure of 32 taels corresponded exactly. There is no record of half chests, but the following information gave some ideas to work on:

(1755)	16 chests	10,030 pieces	Cost 20 taels per chest	26 pieces each
	12 chests	7,944 pieces	Cost 21 taels per chest	662 pieces each
	26 chests	18,166 pieces	Cost 23 taels per chest	698 pieces each

If the *Griffin*'s half chests cost 16 taels each, we decided to work out the average of the above three examples and came up with 662 pieces costing just over 21 taels. We then worked out that 1 tael bought 31.5 pieces and multiplied this by 16 to end up with a half chest containing 504 pieces. Obviously this method is a very simplistic one and as some chests would contain mugs or bowls there would not be so many in these, so we decided to work on the basis of a half chest containing 450 pieces and a whole one 800. This gave a total of 110 whole chests = 88,000 pieces, and 84 half chests = 37,500 pieces, or a grand total of 125,800 pieces of chinaware.

From the diary we were able to form an impression of the difficult working conditions and quite isolated lives which the supracargoes led. Their reward for coping with all the problems caused by the Chinese was a small salary which was boosted by a commission, varying according to their rank in the council, on the proceeds from sales of the cargoes of ships for which they had been responsible. To make life in Canton more financially attractive they were also permitted to send home a small allowance of private trade on each ship and the Company was prepared to advance them sums out of cash at Canton to be paid back in London out of sales. Commission and private trade revenue was credited in an account book and, after several years as a supracargo, a man could become relatively rich.

At the end of 1760 Thomas Lockwood, after a total of twelve years as a supracargo, five of which had been spent continually in Canton, decided to retire. He opted to return on the *Griffin* as Thomas Dethick was the senior commander and his ship would lead the fleet. There is no record of what he loaded on board the ship, however we felt that he had probably accumulated an interesting collection of more valuable merchandise to be sold in London to help finance his retirement, and this prospect added still more interest to the story and the search, especially as we found records for previous years stating he had sent back gold.

We had now amassed a surprisingly large amount of information on the *Griffin*, much more than we could have reasonably expected, as most ships sink without witnesses and often there are no survivors to tell the story. All that remained to investigate in the India Office Library and Records was what happened at the court of inquiry, which we were sure must have been convened, and to see if the Company had attempted to salvage the cargo or had issued a licence to a private individual for this purpose. This information was to be found in the Court minutes, the books kept by the Directors covering all the Company's day-to-day business.

These books run from 1 April to 31 March each year. We knew that the *Suffolk* had been at St Helena in May 1761 and that it took about three months to sail from there to England, so the Court minutes book, reference B.77, for 1761–62 was requested. At the beginning of a meeting held on 23 September 1761 a number of letters were read out to the Directors including ones from:

Thomas Lockwood on board the
    Valentine off Portland   *10 September*

Captain Lewis of the
    Suffolk off Beachy Head   *19 September*

Captain Thomas Debuke of
    Pocock off Dover   *20 September*

Captain William Webber, Jr, of
    Oxford off Beachy Head   *19 September*

and

Captain Thomas Dethick of the *Valentine* relating the particulars of the loss of the *Griffin* in the China Seas.

The Court minutes are completely business like and contain no superfluous comments or sentiment. There was nothing further about the *Griffin*'s loss other than the resolution: 'Referred to Committee of Private Trade to examine into the conduct of Captain Dethick and his officers'. Unfortunately none of the original letters received by the Court survive and, even worse, in 1860, after the Company's records had been passed over to the India Office, it was decided to destroy almost all documents relating to the commercial side of the Company's activities. Presumably the Victorians, with their great imperialist sense of values, considered the trade side of the Company's history rather unsavoury and so consigned all these records to the dump. It does appear that a quantity of this material found its way into private collections and the India Office Library and Records has been given and has purchased a number of disposed archives, but not the reports of the committee of private trade, so it was not possible to read Captain Dethick's account of the wreck. The Court minutes do record that he and the other officers were exonerated, so our previous conclusion that Dalrymple was more to blame than anyone else was upheld to some extent. We then checked the indexes to the Court minutes for the next twenty years and found no further mention of the *Griffin,* so we presumed that no salvage was ever contemplated because, during this search, we did find entries for diving on other wrecks.

It seemed likely that some of the London newspapers might have written something on the *Griffin*'s wreck, so back at the main part of the British Library all the newspapers for September and October were checked. In the London *Evening Chronicle* for 24–26 September was an article which stated that it was an extract of a letter from an officer on board the *Pocock.* Most of what it described confirmed what we already knew from the ships' logs, but added the vital and confusing information that the ship had 'struck on a rock and got off again and lay at anchor in seven fathoms' and that the water had come in so fast that 'they were obliged to cut her cable and let her drive ashore'. This did not seem to make sense. We knew that the Griffin Rocks were at the end of a reef which extended for $2\frac{3}{4}$ miles from Kaludud Island and that the current that night was very strong, about five knots. Both Kris and Franck were able to confirm that in this area it runs roughly north–south, so it seemed unlikely that the stricken ship could have sailed due west to beach on this island. Did this letter mean that she was beached on another part of the reef or did she somehow sail to one of the small islands further south? Was the report simply incorrect or mere sensationalism?

The next problem that this article raised was over the scene next morning. It said that tables, chairs and chests, etc., were floating past the *Pocock*. Her log quite definitely states that this ship was anchored to the west of the *Griffin*, so how did the flotsam float past when the current ran to the south? More exaggeration? We re-read all the logs very carefully and a number of small points which had previously been ignored now seemed to stand out as glaring errors. The *Pocock* said that at dawn Kaludud was east-south-east, the *Griffin* south-east and 'five high rocks about two miles', which we supposed represented the Lakit Islands (some four miles from Griffin Rocks) were south-south-east. This could only mean that the ship was somewhere near the Brutus Reef, about two miles from Griffin Rocks and had got the distance to the 'five high rocks' wrong, unless she had somehow managed to anchor to the south of it, which was considered unlikely. Later in the day, at 4 p.m., the surviving ships were well under way to Sulu, but the *Pocock* made a note '*Griffin* ENE' in her log. Was the ship still visible or was this just a final epitaph?

Modern pilot books did not properly answer the question of possible changes in current direction which would explain the wreckage floating past the *Pocock* and so the Royal Navy Hydrographic Department was consulted. There were some very interesting early documents on sailing directions for this area and we were also able to consult old tables to calculate that there was a full moon on the night the *Griffin* sank and that the tide would have been lower than usual, which helped explain some of the discrepancies in soundings given by the ships. We felt increasingly hopeful that Dalrymple would provide some of the missing details and so headed back to the British Library, where the manuscript room holds a large collection of his original correspondence. This unfortunately revealed nothing other than a passing reference, but the map room did produce one of the most important pieces of evidence so far discovered: a chart prepared by the *Griffin*'s third mate, James Swithin, for Lawrence Sullivan, the chairman of the Company, showing the positions of all the ships. It was very crude, showing islands the wrong shape, out of position, and also not to any scale, but we were able to confirm a number of theories. The chart quite clearly marked the rocks on which the *Griffin* struck. To the south of these was the position of the *Pocock* at anchor and further south and slightly to the east was the place where the *Griffin* actually sank. This chart made the sequence of events look like the *Griffin* freed herself of the reef and was being pushed by the tide while the crew were trying to set a course for a larger island called Pilas. What was totally confusing was the lack of scale, the presence of rocks which simply do not exist according to modern charts, and the complete omission of some islands. Finding this chart was fascinating, but it did complicate matters. It was, however, better to be confused than to go ahead with a search on the assumption that the wreck was to be found somewhere on the reef near Kaludud.

Our information was now virtually complete and there was certainly enough to be able to narrow down the search to an area of five square miles, most of which was in the lee of Kaludud and could thus be discounted; the final area was a triangle of just over $2\frac{1}{2}$ square miles. This was still a much larger zone than we would have liked, but quite feasible.

This research had taken several months and during this time Franck had been busy assembling his team of divers, whilst Kris and Terry were working on the *Load Star* and putting together the vast amount of necessary equipment. With the sheaf of papers which had been assembled from the research, the National Museum in Manila upgraded the permit from only exploration to full excavation. The whole team was then transferred to Zamboanga City, the capital of Mindanao, and the delicate political situation there soon became apparent. It seemed that the Muslim Filipinos had the upper hand in what was virtually a civil war against the Government. The last thing we wanted was to be attacked by pirates whilst on the site and in this part of the world documents from a Government a long way off mean nothing. Our agent in Manila, Lomar, suggested employing a military unit to provide protection, but Franck made contact with a local Muslim commander in Zamboanga who ran a 'security company' and agreed, on the basis of having a potential enemy on our side, to employ a number of his men as permanent guards on board the ship.

Once the *Load Star* had finished her sea trials after the refit, Franck set off for the search area in early June. His assistants had already prepared a large-scale map of the area and divided it into a grid, with horizontal and vertical lines forming 250 square metre blocks. These were to be the directions for the search and the *Load Star* was to spend a month sailing first up and down and then across every line, dragging a magnetometer behind her.

Proton magnetometers (we used two Elsec 7706 models) detect disturbances in the Earth's magnetic field caused by any ferrous metal objects (which have their own magnetic field) interfering with the Earth's and are used to detect any iron based objects on or under the sea bed. These might be pieces of iron from a shipwreck, but could equally be lumps of iron ore bearing volcanic rock, and it requires a high degree of expertise to understand the read-out, which is in units of one millionth of a gamma, the measurement of magnetic strength. Unfortunately, Sangboy is a volcanic island, so the whole zone was affected by this and, to make our job even more difficult, it soon became apparent that the entire area was subject to highly irregular currents changing 180 degrees in a day, sometimes very strong and at other times non-existent. The magnetometer had to be dragged on a cable about fifty feet behind the ship so as not to be affected by the iron on board and, with the current, it was easily dragged off course, as could the ship be, so a separate fixed positioning system called transponder motorola was installed on three separate islands within the search area. On our visit to place one on Kaludud, we discovered the island was a base for the Communist National Peoples Army (NPA), which was a sobering prospect, but, fortunately, the Muslims are on reasonably friendly terms with this group. The instruments continually fed positioning information into a computer on the bridge and the course could be corrected so that her location was always known to within two yards. This system is far more accurate than the satellite navigation equipment on board as it is intended to show a position at sea, when an error of fifty yards does not matter.

The magnetometer was attached to a printer on board and this churned out reams of paper covered in graph lines as the instrument monitored the magnetic field. Any ferrous object produced an anomaly which made the highly sensitive needle jump. This information then had to be interpreted in an attempt to decide what each anomaly reading represented

Sidescan sonar was also used but this, which produces soundwaves and builds up a picture of the sea floor, was not of great benefit as the bottom was only sand and no part of the wreck was visible. A Sidescan sonar picture of the bottom shows shadows caused by irregularities such as rocks or a mound caused by a shipwreck and we found it just confirmed what an initial dive had already revealed – that the search zone was an area of undulating sand dunes.

Each night Franck plotted the information produced by the magnetometer on to the chart of the area along the line which the ship had covered that day. After about two weeks, the *Load Star* had covered all the north–south lines and the various anomalies were marked. It was only when she began to sail east–west that some of the marks already in place were confirmed by another jump on the graph paper as they passed over an intersection in the grid. This double referencing was fascinating and slowly several areas of anomalies began to take shape. These were again surveyed in more detail. One place showed several high readings (60 gamma) and Franck decided to call Kris out of Cebu, where he had been collecting still more equipment. He showed Kris the graph paper and the two of them went over the information individually, plotting each anomaly on an unmarked chart. Kris's findings agreed with Franck's and both of them knew that it could only mean that there was something very significant down there. The search was over.

CHAPTER 6

The Dive

To make absolutely sure, the *Load Star* went back yet again to the high anomaly area. The magnetometer was put out for the third time and they did a couple of short runs. The same results came up. Kris and Franck both dived down only to be greeted with a view of sand as far as the eye could see. Finding the *Griffin* was obviously not going to be an easy task and the time had come for some serious work.

Further detailed inspection of the survey results revealed two distinct roughly parallel lines of anomalies running about 600 metres apart. These were not actually continuous runs but rather a series of disjointed readings which, when ruled through, formed a line. Sadly, nowhere was there a large distortion which could be construed to represent the ship, but it was decided to make the first dive at the spot which had initially alerted Franck. Strangely, this had been noticed on the very first day of the survey, but had been disregarded as a disturbance – it would have been too much to expect, even for the most optimistic among us, to find the wreck on day one. Our six divers had been joined by two from the National Museum and were waiting at Zamboanga for the *Sea Wind* to pick them up. After a couple of exploratory dives, during which nothing whatsoever was seen, it became obvious that whatever we had found was buried at some depth and would only be revealed by digging a test hole.

The solution was to make a couple of airlifts. These are simply gigantic vacuum cleaners which ran off the ship's two generators and sucked away the sand. It took the chief diver, Gilbert, a day to design the system he wanted and then our welder, René, was set to work. The finished product was a thirty-foot length of PVC pipe with four feet of eight-inch steel piping attached to one end. In the steel section René welded a downwards facing valve, into which a two-inch rubber hose could be clipped. The suction pipes ran from the generators on deck to a buoy and then down to the bottom in galvanized iron. This contained the valves to turn the airlift

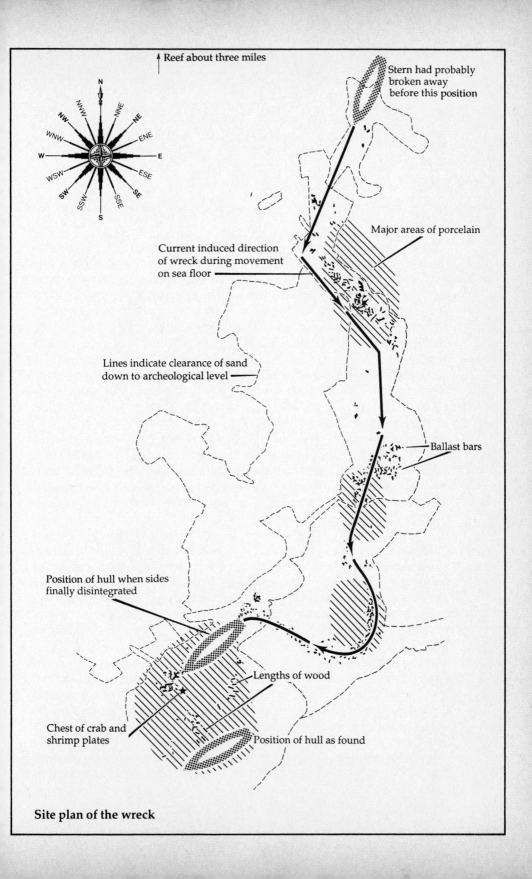

Reef about three miles

N
NNW N NNE
NW   NE
WNW   ENE
W   E
WSW   ESE
SW   SE
SSW S SSE

Stern had probably
broken away
before this position

Major areas of porcelain

Current induced direction
of wreck during movement
on sea floor

Lines indicate clearance of sand
down to archeological level

Ballast bars

Position of hull when sides
finally disintegrated

Lengths of wood

Chest of crab and
shrimp plates

Position of hull as found

Site plan of the wreck

on and off, and, because of its rigidity, the two-inch rubber pipes attached to the airlift came out of these valves allowing the diver to move about at will. The downward angle of the attachment at the base of the airlift was to prevent sand being sucked into the main system rather than up the PVC tube, and the diver held the device just under the coupling, about six inches to a foot from the nozzle, which was covered with mesh to prevent anything larger than sand being sucked away. René made two eight-inch airlifts, two of six inches, and one with a four-inch diameter.

The area we were concentrating on was one of high sand dunes rising up to twelve feet above the otherwise featureless flat bottom. It seemed possible that these could be covering a wreck, so the first excavation with the airlift was made in a valley between two dunes. By doing this it was hoped that as little sand as possible would have to be shifted before arriving at the archaeological level, the layer at which material from a shipwreck is located.

This appeared to be quite simple. If a dune was concealing a wreck then, as each of these was about twelve feet high, the level would only be a foot or two down; also the water was forty feet deep, so a dive could last for two to three hours and, including the thirty minutes which would have to be spent at twenty feet to allow for decompression, this gave plenty of time to do good work on each descent. There is nothing more frustrating than to be working in deeper water and having to spend so much time avoiding the bends that only twenty or thirty minutes can be spent on the actual site. The bends are a condition every diver fears: cramps caused by nitrogen, which is absorbed underwater, being released too quickly into the bloodstream and can actually be fatal if not treated. The *Load Star* had a decompression chamber on her deck, but, as the water we were diving in was relatively shallow, this was fortunately never needed and all that the divers were required to do was to wait for the prescribed periods at twenty and ten feet respectively before surfacing. From the ship we hung coloured cards printed with the British Sub-Aqua Club tables showing the times to wait at each depth.

The divers worked in shifts for two days without finding anything. They sucked the sand up in long sweeping motions so that nothing of any interest would be disturbed and this enabled them to cover an area of three to four feet in a single sweep. This was by far the best method, as digging a smaller hole would have been pointless because the surrounding sand would simply fall into it and, in any case, nobody would be able to see properly what was going on. They dug far deeper than even the most pessimistic on board had

China Sea Explorer (*right*) and *Ocean Explorer* at the site.

On deck before a dive: (*left to right*) Tom Steider, Kris Shaffer and Franck Goddio.

Uncovering the first signs of the *Griffin* with the airlift.

Many pieces of porcelain were broken.

Part of a chest of dinner plates: a diver making detailed notes prior to removing them. (*Below*) More of the chest has been exposed and some pieces have been bagged.

The 'crab and prawn' plates *in situ*: the chest of plates 'looked like a piece of machinery' when first uncovered. (*Below*) One of the loose plates.

To the south of the 'crab chest' we found the first pieces of wood from the *Griffin*'s hull. In the background is the chest, boxed and ready to take to the surface. (*Below*) A section of the hull exposed to show the futtocks protruding from each side of the keel.

Kris and Penny Shaffer examining a day's find.

Georges Pfeiffer made scale drawings of every different piece and pattern found.

From the Manila exhibition, a diarama showing the ship on site with divers working; the dunes give some idea of the immense quantity of sand removed.

Part of one of the rooms in Evelyne Jay's house in Manila full of the *Griffin*'s porcelain after restoration and cataloguing.

One of the display cases at the Manila exhibition containing a range of tea bowls and saucers with some of Georges's drawings.

From the Manila exhibition, a selection of wine bottles, clay pipes, shoe buckles and an ivory fan found on the wreck.

predicted. At the beginning of the third day the trench was over twelve feet deep and six feet long and many of the team felt that nothing could possibly be buried that far down. Then, just before lunchtime, a diver emerged from the water, his arm extended above his head. He was holding a small piece of blue and white porcelain. It was not a whole plate, but large enough for the typical mid-eighteenth-century design of a pine tree and crane to be immediately recognizable. The six divers waiting topside broke all records for donning face-masks and tanks and soon two more shards were uncovered at the same level.

They had been discovered exactly fifteen feet down in the sand, or fifty-five feet from the surface, where the fine sand cover gave way to a layer of coarser material mixed with small pieces of coral. The spot was carefully marked and measured before a much more delicate examination began. Nothing else was found in this section and an airlift was brought in to take out even more sand. By the time it had penetrated a further five feet without finding anything, it seemed likely that the archaeological level was indeed where the three shards had been found.

There was no diving the next day. A few had sore heads after the previous night's celebration, but most were intently studying the comparisons between the magnetometer read-out and our chart plotting the anomalies. The shards had been discovered along a line which extended for some distance north-north-east and south-south-west. Next day the first team took down stakes and a length of cord, and marked this direction in the sand before choosing another valley along the line about twenty feet from where the shards had been found. It took another two days to dig a similar trench down to the archaeological level, but the work was rewarded by finding two twisted pieces of lead sheet of the type which might have lined a tea chest. The next hole exposed what looked like a lump of coral about two feet long with numerous porcelain shards and complete bowls concreted on to it. Closer inspection on board revealed that this was actually an iron ballast bar with the name Elkridge cast into it. In the main, only European ships carried iron ballast, the ones from India used stones or bricks and the presence of the English foundry name confirmed that we had found an East Indiamen. We had found the *Griffin*.

The wreck was obviously there somewhere, but it was daunting to realize that to find it we would have to shift the sand dunes and then dig down another fifteen feet – up to twenty-seven feet altogether. The first week's work had also been complicated by the current which, when strong at night, pushed so much sand back into the excavation that each morning several hours' work was necessary to return to the previous day's level and conversely, if it was not strong enough, the sand coming from the top of the airlift during excavation would fall straight down. Ideal daytime conditions were with a current of about five to six knots and, when this was the case, the sand coming out of the airlifts made them look like great chimneys belching out smoke into a fresh breeze. It would have been easy if the current was constant or even followed a predictable pattern, but it changed every day, sometimes strong, other times weak and occasionally non-existent, and virtually never from the same direction on consecutive days. Generally, however, it flowed from roughly north to south in the mornings and eased in strength about noon before beginning to turn, eventually going around 180 degrees. It was at least fortunate that diving was possible most mornings, but after the current began to turn the slack water might last an hour or all afternoon; one never knew what it was going to do. When the conditions were good, the divers had to literally climb down the galvanized iron pipes which fed the airlifts or be blown away by what they described as the 'wind'. Fortunately the holes they dug acted as a break and there was no current once they were in them and at work.

During this time the fishermen who live a subsistence existence on the nearby islands of Kaludud and Dassalan became curious as to what we were up to and gathered around the *Load Star* in their outrigger canoes, *bankas*. As pieces of porcelain began to come up they soon realized that we were looking for a shipwreck and one of the more forthcoming ones of the group came on board and said that, for the equivalent of US$250, he would show us the cannons. Filipino fishermen have almost no money at all and the average wage in Manila is about US$2.00 a day, so this sum would have probably been enough to keep him for several years. We had no hesitation in saying that the money (which was produced) would be paid, but only after he had shown us the guns and not before as he wished. He pushed off, crestfallen and muttering, but we thought an investigation of the area around the reef would not be wasted time just in case there was something in his story. Franck and the guards made a couple of exploratory dives in difficult conditions, but did not see any sign of the guns or the usual tell-tale shards and, convinced that the *Griffin* lay near where we were working, he ordered diving to recommence.

Gradually a pattern of diving was established. Our eight divers were divided into pairs and each team could go down twice a day for between two and three hours, depending on how experienced at breathing they were. Diving was controlled almost completely by the vagaries of the current. The first pair normally went down at about 6 a.m., just after dawn. The second team dived about 8 a.m. and they might overlap the others or meet them at the twenty feet mark, but there was little point in having more than two divers working at one time as only two airlifts were in use. The four others were brought into action for the delicate or slower work, but, when the major job of exposing the archaeological level was going on, they remained on deck unused. Everyday at slack water a solo diver would go down, generally either Franck or Frederick Osada, and would work on measuring or photography when the conditions did not favour the airlifts. The third team dived at 10 a.m., and the last, providing the current was holding, went at midday. If conditions were still good in the afternoon, the performance would be repeated, with overlaps, the teams diving again at 2, 3.30, 4 and 6 p.m.

Diving began in early August. By the end of September the divers had moved an enormous amount of sand and were well on the way to revealing the last track of the *Griffin*. The path they exposed was nine feet wide and nearly 3,000 feet long, littered with debris which had spilled out of the hull as it was dragged along the sea bed by the current. At first the finds were sparsely distributed but as time went on, more and more pieces were uncovered along the path. Every piece of porcelain, whether it was a shard or complete specimen was gathered after being carefully plotted on the master chart. Frederick mapped the bottom and used the line which had been put down when the first finds were made as his baseline from which to make all calculations. The first view a diver had of the sea floor was that of a giant chessboard, crisscrossed with ropes which measured out one square metre areas.

When mapping the site, we were disadvantaged in that there were absolutely no fixed points in the form of rocks or other immovable objects which could be used for trilateration, the process of measuring two points from one fixed spot in order to draw a scale diagram. Every morning the sand looked different after the current had deposited more material and moved it around, so the only solution was to construct a huge grid, which was duplicated to scale on the chart on board. After we left the site, certain very long marker poles were left buried deep in the sand so that any future investigators would be able to reconstruct our grid exactly. The process of mapping the site was a slow one and occupied one complete dive each day. Everything which had been exposed was left lying in the exact position in which it had been uncovered and each grid square was photographed after important or interesting pieces had been marked. Only then was everything gathered up. This means that, should we ever wish to, an entire square could be exactly reproduced as it was found. Specimens of the sand were also taken for future analysis.

With such a large site, far bigger than we ever imagined, costs were accruing every day without finding the actual wreck and so, in October, it was decided that, as there were so many shards, we would discontinue collecting these until the hull was found and only perfect pieces of porcelain were brought up thereafter. So far we had found ballast bars, ballast stones, pieces of lead and a large amount of porcelain, but no timbers or anything belonging to the crew. There were also a couple of old broken cannons which were listed in the *Griffin*'s log as having been loaded in Bombay: 'October 26 [1759]. Took on board 19 tons of Ballast and 9 old iron guns on account of the Honourable Company.' The cannons were in very poor condition with no discernible marks on them and we wondered if they might have been captured during the campaign against the Mahrattas which had ended only shortly before the *Griffin* arrived in India.

Work continued on the track during October and November. By the beginning of December our excavation was over a mile long and zig-zagged several times, showing where the tides had changed the ship's course on the bottom. From our knowledge of the current, we knew that we must have exposed about a week of continual movement of the ship underwater, but had no way of knowing if our path began where the ship had finally sunk or if it extended further north. We only followed the track to the south as it obviously led in this direction and finding the wreck took top priority.

During these months of work, the divers' spirits remained high. At first, when the track was weak, there were few perfect pieces, but now each dive revealed about ten good pieces of porcelain per diver, which they would put into mesh bags and bring up once the photography was finished. Sometimes larger quantities were found and these were stacked into baskets with plenty of sand as padding and raised to the surface with a lift-bag. This is a balloon that can be filled with air from the diver's tank and is an effective method of bringing quite heavy consignments up. In these ways about 150 pieces each day came on to the ship, where our ceramics conservator, Evelyne Jay, proceeded to put them through a number of tanks to remove the ingrained salt. Also on board was Georges Pfeiffer, who made beautiful life-size drawings of every new design and shape.

When not underwater, the Museum divers worked on cataloguing everything and, as the National Museum looked on the work as a unique opportunity to train their staff in the field, we had a continual turnover of people and we were able to both help them and, in turn, learn something of Filipino culture.

Fortunately, almost all of the complete pieces of porcelain which were found were in good condition and not at all covered in marine encrustations, so they must have been completely covered by sand within a day or two of falling out of the ship. This had preserved the glaze beautifully and the blue and white pieces were perfect. Unfortunately, the rarer enamelled pieces had lost virtually all trace of their decoration, it having been eroded by the sand and eaten away by bacteria. Had these specimens, which often made up the bulk of the private trade, been exposed and covered by calcareous concretions they would have been better preserved. We had great hopes, once it was established that the ship was not on the reef, of finding the hull in good condition and had anticipated finding both a quantity of porcelain and personal effects *in situ*. As work progressed, however, the sheer quantity of pieces being uncovered became worrying and we were fearful that the reef might have literally ripped open the *Griffin*'s hull and her cargo gradually dropped out. Several European East Indiamen have been discovered but, so far as we knew to that date, no one had found the wreck of one lost on the return voyage from China and we looked forward to learning not only more about the construction of these vessels but also to investigating how the sailors were affected by having been in China through their souvenirs and adoption of Chinese clothing as their own wore out.

A Dutch East Indiaman, the *Amsterdam*, which sank on the English coast near Hastings, was built in the same year as the *Griffin* and was subjected to an intensive examination in the early 1970s. We knew that the English ships had only one gun deck, not two like the *Amsterdam*, but, other than contemporary guidelines issued to shipwrights and paintings, we had no detailed evidence of what they actually looked like and how each part of the ship was divided and used. The *Amsterdam*'s construction and appearance was closely studied and is excellently reported by Peter Marsden in his book *The Wreck of the Amsterdam*, so a comparison in merchant ship building and design techniques between Holland and England would have been very interesting.

During our excavation, Kris had to make several trips to Hong Kong and, after one, brought back a copy of a new book by Christiaan

Jorg, *The Geldermalsen, History and Porcelain.* This is the story of a
Dutch ship which sank on the way back from China in 1752. It had
been discovered by Michael Hatcher near Singapore a year previously, apparently in a good state of preservation. Jorg made several
comments about the lack of archaeological study of this wreck and,
while we were envious of his having beaten us to it, so to speak,
and the quantity of porcelain, it served to strengthen our desire to
find the *Griffin* and learn as much as possible from her.

Whilst the divers were busy under water, those permanently on
board were also kept fully occupied. By mid-November we had been
on site for five months and various logistical problems needed sorting
out. The *Sea Wind* was too small to carry a large quantity of provisions
and spent almost all her time going back and forth to Zamboanga,
a six-hour sail. Our supplies of meat came in bulk from Labuan in
Malaysia, which was a round trip of a week and, as this run was
necessary every six weeks, sometimes we were without fresh vegetables. As a result Kris decided to bring another ship, the 160-foot
Ocean Explorer on to the site. She is equipped with very large tanks
for extra water and fuel, her freezers meant that the Labuan run
was less frequent and the *Load Star*'s occasional problem of over-
crowding when official visitors came to the site was solved. Fresh
goods still had to come from Zamboanga and it was decided to use
the guard's boat for this, seeing as it was making regular visits to
the site in any case.

The guards were a most peculiar group. Initially they lived in a
tent at the *Load Star*'s bow and were not permitted inside the ship,
then, when the *Ocean Explorer* arrived, they moved across to live
on her deck, but continued to come over every day. We would much
have preferred to be without them but, in an area where pirates
are a fact of life and there is so much civil unrest, it would have
been foolish not to have had some protection. The divers were fortunately able to ignore them to a large extent, but our crew had day-to-
day dealings which often proved most unsatisfactory.

Mindanao is an island whose population is largely descended from
Malay Muslims and the Spanish missionaries never made great
inroads in their attempts to convert the people to Catholicism. There
is a powerful lobby for independence from the Philippines and the
Muslims actively involved in the illegal militaristic wing of this
struggle are known as Moros. To complicate matters, there is also
a Communist group called the NPA (National People's Army) who
are engaged in their own campaign against the Government and,
although they do not fight the Moros, there is a distinctly uneasy

feeling when the two organizations meet. Our guards were Muslims, but belonged to an officially licenced security company and were, therefore, allowed to carry guns. What they did when not guarding us we never enquired or, indeed, wanted to know.

We knew that the pirates, also Muslims, had fast *bankas* with two powerful outboard motors and mounted 50-calibre machine-guns. They prey on shipping, run extortion rackets with fishermen and are involved in smuggling from Malaysia, all in all a most unpleasant bunch whose boats could out run and out shoot the Philippine Naval Coast Guard vessels. Thanks to our guards we never saw one during our entire time on the site. They were also useful when it came to coming into and leaving Zamboanga. On leaving a port you have to state where the vessel is going so that the right forms can be filled in for customs and the destination port informed; as we were effectively going nowhere this caused the bureaucrats much perplexity until the guard commander had a word and sorted it all out.

These were the positive aspects of their presence. The negative side was, apart from them being a lazy rabble who were always in the way, every time their boat arrived, which just happened to coincide with meal times, it brought large numbers of people, all of whom demanded food and roamed over the ship at will. Whenever anything they wanted was refused, there was much obvious cleaning and pointing of guns and general sabre rattling. Once the *Load Star*'s captain, Tom Steider, was even threatened with a pistol.

There was also the importance of keeping the ship constantly above the site to consider and this became a serious problem as the current could drag her fifty feet in only a few days and the satellite navigation system would not be able to detect the change. Deep sand does not provide a firm anchorage at the best of times and with the current as well, a special arrangement called a six-point anchoring system using $1\frac{1}{2}$-ton ex-Navy special sand anchors with very wide flukes was devised by the *Ocean Explorer*'s captain, Tim Burrell. These were spread at all points of the compass on $\frac{3}{4}$-inch chains up to 400 metres from the ship with an arrangement of three at each end of the *Load Star*. The anchor chains were additionally weighted down with concrete blocks, each of about one cubic metre, and it was hoped that this system would hold the ship absolutely rigid. It did not, and about once every two weeks work would have to stop for a whole day while the three anchors which had dragged – pulling the ship towards the other three – would have to be brought up, the slack tightened and then the three which had moved were repositioned. The fact that we had to do this, despite having taken such elaborate precautions, gave us some idea of what the *Griffin* must have gone through once she sank and it was no wonder that her track was so long.

In early December all the anchors had to come up when a typhoon changed direction and began to head towards us. Both ships headed for Pilas Island, twelve miles to the south-east, where, according to the pilot book there is a good safe anchorage. The people we found there rarely had visitors and were friendly, all participating in the party which we held one night on the beach. Many of the divers had not touched dry land for six weeks and were glad of the break, which was a nice change from their usual routine of up at 5.30 a.m. followed by work all day and collapsing exhausted into bed about 9.30 p.m. We stayed for four or five days until the typhoon once again changed course and, on returning to the site had a nasty shock when a coast guard boat came alongside and told us Pilas was 'off limits'. Why this was we never discovered, but for the next couple of months the same ship came along regularly to inspect our permit.

There was no damage from the storm and we were soon back at work. On 11 December, divers Patrick Lize and Tom Whittier were working as usual on the track, which for some time had been heading west-south-west, a direction which had not previously been observed. There had been a large deposit of ballast bars and porcelain at the end of a north-west track before the course veered in this direction and, even though they were obviously following the right path, only a few pieces had been found in the previous two days. They thought the track might have turned south again and made a couple of exploratory test holes without finding anything. The air-lifts were working on what was to be the last of these deviations when suddenly a most unusual serrated object, which looked like a piece of machinery, was uncovered. It was heavily encrusted and quite unlike anything either of them had seen before, but they continued to suck away the sand. Soon the object revealed itself as a virtually complete case of octagonal dinner plates with a rare crab and prawn design in blue and white. The first serrated appearance had been a row of sixty flat edges of these plates. There were three entire rows and about half of a fourth, with several more stacked at right angles to the main body. It looked as if one corner of the crate must have split open when it hit bottom, spilling part of the contents which were now missing, but one plate was lying lose and Patrick swam up with it. The customary break for thirty minutes at twenty feet was probably the longest half hour of his life. There was some surprise on board as he swam towards the ship, as he had only been down for ninety minutes, but when the plate came out of his bag and the discovery related there was a second rush of divers, all eager to see for themselves the first complete chest, which they had each dreamt of finding.

Frederick had quite a job clearing away the press of divers surrounding it before motioning to Patrick to replace the plate exactly as it had been found so that he could photograph the area. While he had been alone, Tom had carefully dug away more sand and had found most of the original wood, all beautifully dovetailed, still in position. The strangest feature, however, was the row of plates at right angles to the rest. We had always assumed that each chest was specially constructed to fit around a given quantity of plates, but here was evidence that the chest had been delivered empty and, after four rows had been packed in there was still a bit of extra room which had also been filled up.

It would have been tragic if this unique discovery had broken up on its way to the surface, which was the risk with using an air-bag, so a special casing was made on deck and lowered down. Once in position, a flooring was slid underneath and the case was brought to the surface by the ship's crane. This was exactly the type of thing we had been searching for from the very beginning and the crew gathered around in much the same way as the divers had done when it was underwater. Evelyne may have had to chastise people for attempting to touch the plates, but everyone was in high spirits that night.

During the next week leading up to Christmas the airlifts exposed a large area surrounding the chest and more plates and ballast bars were found along the original west-south-west course which Tom and Patrick had been working on before deviating. The finds petered out after about thirty metres and a trench was dug fifteen metres to the north-west, but without success. Trying to decide which direction the path would take after the trail disappeared was always extremely difficult and much exploration was done in the wrong direction. It was easy to see from the zigzags on the main chart how the hull was pushed in different directions as the current changed, but it must have been as erratic then as it is now and so it was impossible to say that the track in each direction would be the same length, nor indeed did we know how long in time each section represented.

Eventually the only solution was to begin digging in all directions from the position of the chest and this decision paid off in spectacular fashion on 16 December, when the first timbers were uncovered.

There were a number of pieces, each about eight feet long and a foot wide, and once squared off. They could have only come from the ship. As more and more were found while the divers pushed the front to the south-south-east the site looked as though someone had dismantled the joists from an old house and thrown all the wood out of the windows. Planks lay in all directions, some resting across others, other pieces lying by themselves. Just what part of the ship they came from was a mystery then, but it seemed that the hull could not be far away. Each stage of the dive so far had been slow and painstaking with regular halts for measurement and photography, but there was now no stopping the divers as they worked away at the eighteen foot high wall of sand. A few days later the hull was found. At first all that could be seen were several pieces of wood lying side by side. This was nothing new, other pieces were in the same configuration, but as more was uncovered three pieces became four, then five, and eventually a dozen or more were there, all joined together. There were also hundreds of pieces of porcelain, but these, for the first time, were largely ignored.

As each dive was completed, Frederick or one of the others took photographs and the smaller airlifts were brought down to ensure that nothing moved while the sand was being taken away. Uncovering the entire hull took over a week, but it was the best Christmas present anyone could have had. At the end we found it was 29 metres or 96.6 feet long and appeared to be the major part of the keel with ribs coming out at right angles and covered on both sides by planking. On top of the outside planking was a second layer, making a double skin. All the wood was in good recognizable condition considering it had been underwater for 225 years and this was ascribed to the fact that it had been quickly buried in the sand. Had she lain on the reef and in water, the *Griffin* would soon have been eaten away to nothing by teredo worms and other sea life which flourish in these warm waters. The wood looked as if it had been charred by burning, with deep lines running along the grain and in the main had a somewhat withered appearance, but the general shape of each piece was clear. Once all the sand had been cleared several large chunks of coral lay on top of the timbers, a testimony to the *Griffin*'s fate.

The keel was the longest single piece of wood, and at one end extended some six feet from the main body of ribs and planks. As we knew that it had originally been 105 feet long, it seemed that we had found most of the hull as far as the bow and that the stern section had somehow broken away at about the position of the mizzen-mast. Nothing remained of the sides of the ship; these must

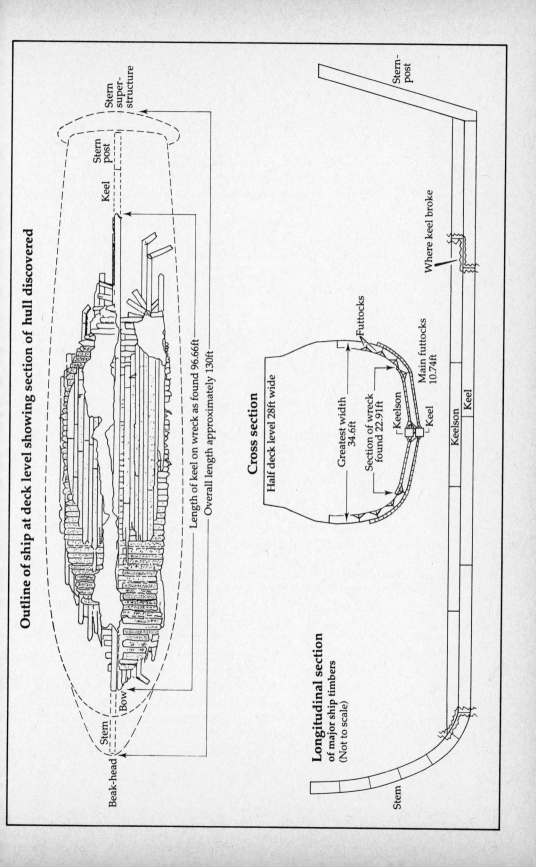

Outline of ship at deck level showing section of hull discovered

Stern super-structure

Stern post

Keel

Length of keel on wreck as found 96.66ft

Overall length approximately 130ft

Bow

Stem

Beak-head

Cross section

Half deck level 28ft wide

Greatest width 34.6ft

Section of wreck found 22.91ft

Futtocks

Main futtocks 10.74ft

Keelson

Keel

Longitudinal section
of major ship timbers
(Not to scale)

Stern-post

Where keel broke

Keel

Keelson

Stem

have broken apart during the time she was rolling about on the bottom or as a result of the current once the wreck was at rest. It was disappointing not to have all the ship, especially as the stern contained the most important cabins and therefore the most interesting artefacts. We also felt that it would have been the most heavily ballasted part of the ship and would have held more porcelain, but finding anything at all was preferable to finding her eaten away and overgrown by coral, which is the fate of most wrecks in this part of the world. Whatever people thought privately, the thrill of the find was enough to keep everyone occupied for the remainder of December and January. Around the hull and especially in the area where the stern had broken away were piles of porcelain, ballast bars and lead sheeting from tea chests. Indeed, whenever anything was moved, clouds of tea leaves floated up and several blocks of compressed tea were found. We also found some clay pipes, shoe buckles, several wine bottles and a broken wine glass, but these were the full extent of the crew's possessions for the time being. On the night of 20 January, the anniversary of the *Griffin*'s loss, we held a party on board and it was strange to think of the ship exposed beneath us.

By February the *Load Star* was coming up for its ninth month at sea and was in need of some work on a slipway, so it was decided to give the team a month's well-earned holiday whilst the ship went into the yards in Cebu. Here her name was changed to a more appropriate one for the type of work she was now doing: *China Sea Explorer*. The *Ocean Explorer* remained on site with the guards and a skeleton crew to maintain our claim to the wreck, while nearly everyone else flew home to a cold European winter. Kris and Franck took the opportunity to sit down with the researchers and several other people experienced in salvage to work out the next phase of the operation: finding the stern. One of the problems with seeking advice is that one ends up with ten different suggestions and this is exactly what happened to us. Opinions varied dramatically. One person thought the stern must be very close to the section we had already found, some thought it must be on the reef, and one opined that the course of the ship, according to the log, placed her point of impact as the Brutus Reef, about two miles west of Griffin Rocks. Others thought the ship had long ago been plundered and the most pessimistic view of all was that the rest of the ship had broken up completely and the remaining contents were scattered for miles over the ocean floor.

Back on site again in March the divers were set to work clearing away the fine layer of sand which had covered the exposed track and hull, whilst Franck and some others went up to the Griffin Rocks for the second time and to Brutus Reef to look for clues. On Brutus he found an eighteenth-century anchor which he believed belonged to either the *Valentine* or *Oxford,* but nothing else. Further investigation of the reef around Griffin Rocks was difficult due to the presence of the NPA encampment on Kaludud.

These findings convinced him that the ship had cleared herself off the reef and drifted some distance before sinking. This view was supported by the report from an officer of the *Pocock* which had been printed in a London paper and the rough chart prepared for the Company's chairman which had been found during the first phase of research. Franck therefore decided to concentrate the search to the south of what we had already found.

Within a week this decision appeared to have been correct as a second complete case was uncovered. It contained almost 1,000 saucers. This was an exciting find, but even more important was that the wooden surround, which once again was in good condition, was etched with the initials T. D. and underneath G. This could only stand for Thomas Dethick, the *Griffin's* captain, and it was our first really positive identification of the wreck, even though everything else had pointed to it being the *Griffin* and there was no doubt in anyone's mind that this was the ship. The chest once again was not made to fit the saucers and, like the first one, had probably been thrown out of the hull when the ship finally came to rest as it was found only a few metres away.

This new discovery fired everyone's enthusiasm and work progressed over a wide front for several weeks, again, without finding anything except the odd broken piece. It was time for a rethink. The hull had been moving west-south-west before turning south to her last resting place, with the bow facing east-north-east. It seemed possible that the tide might have turned again to west-south-west, so for a further month the excavation was extended in that direction without success.

It was now June and we had been working on the *Griffin* for a year and had spent about US$1 million. There had been great highs of excitement and much disappointment. Now everyone on board was depressed. The divers could hardly even bring themselves to play with the magnetic chess set suspended at the twenty-feet mark under the *China Sea Explorer.* Two months of work without finding anything is a long time and so Kris decided to call in a company from Singapore called Guardline Surveys, who promised to supply even more powerful equipment than the instruments we had used a year previously. Whilst their ship ploughed up and down, Frederick took the opportunity to try out a new method of photographing the hull which he had been experimenting with. The best image of an archaeological site such as a shipwreck is a photomosaic which can not only show a much larger area but also places everything perfectly in relation. The *Griffin's* hull had presented him with some special problems, mainly due to the current blowing away a diver with a camera even though it was much reduced in the huge depression we had made; any movement of the tripod, no matter how slight, would destroy the continuity of taking a number of shots from the same height and exact distance apart. Fred had also decided that he wanted to create an image of the hull as it actually was, not covered in squares of string and plastic tags as it had been during the investigation and measurement stages.

The device he designed consisted of a ten-metre aluminium pole with a movable carriage underneath, on to which two cameras could be fixed an equal distance apart from each other. This was then suspended at a constant height of three metres from the hull by two tripods placed on the baseline, which was now the only piece of string left. After each photograph the cameras could be moved a measured distance along the pole and, with five changes in position of the whole apparatus, the entire length and breadth of the hull was recorded. In the end forty photographs were pieced together to form a most impressive and successful photomosaic.

The Guardline people finished their survey at the end of June and the results were analysed. Franck had asked them to extend their search further to the south than our original survey had covered but nothing which, even in our wildest imaginations, could represent the stern was found. Nor were any of the cannons located.

Diving continued during July and August with test holes of one square metre being dug down to the archaeological level in a number of places up to several hundred metres from the hull, going in all directions south of an east–west axis without finding anything. Some of the other divers worked on taking specimens for future laboratory study from different parts of the hull and removed one rib to look at the method used for attaching the outer timbers.

On 28 August we decided to leave the site, vowing to return one day and find all the missing pieces.

During the dive we moved an estimated 500,000 tons of sand and were under water for a total of 5,317 hours. In many ways it was a difficult operation. For a start, we commenced work without being able to see anything. The unpredictable current meant that it was extremely difficult to adhere to a proper schedule and, overall, probably several weeks of work was lost because of this. Shifting sand also meant that much excavation had to be done twice and poor visibility often slowed down work. We do not know of any other wreck that has been found buried so deep; finding the hull was a major achievement in itself which was compounded by the fact that it did not show up on the magnetometer survey, being bereft of any significant quantity of metalwork and cannons.

There were great moments: the discovery of the first shard; un-covering the track with a hope and a prayer that the ship was under the next dune; the two chests of porcelain and, of course, the hull itself. Being on the site on the anniversary of the *Griffin*'s loss was also a moving experience for, by coincidence, there was a full moon that night and conditions were almost identical. For Captain Tom Steider holding the *Griffin*'s original log when he came to London in February was an emotional moment.

There were also great disappointments. We had hoped to find the complete wreck, but it was a marvellous achievement to find anything at all. When the second survey failed to produce the evidence we sought, morale visibly dropped and it was for the best that work stopped when it did because carelessness under water can be fatal.

The *Griffin*'s wreck remains where it has done since 1761. It is a national historical monument of the Philippines.

CHAPTER 7

Sea, Sand and Porcelain

As the *China Sea Explorer* sailed slowly up towards Batangas, the main port for Manila, it seemed somehow strange and yet rather wonderful to know that concealed beneath her decks in a large storage chamber under the bridge was the *Griffin*, or at least her cargo, pieces from her hull and some of her sailors' possessions. Those on board, both divers and crew, had lived with the *Griffin* for up to fourteen months and no one had failed to be infected by the tragic image of the empty ship being relentlessly dragged across the bottom by the might of the sea and gradually breaking up. Yet nobody was sad to leave. Some dreamt of future ski-ing holidays or sipping long cool cocktails; there was no desire to go out and lie in the sun and heat: that had been their life for over a year. Many had neglected businesses to return to, others just yearned for a long rest, but the *Griffin*'s draw was such that everyone wanted to go back one day to find the elusive stern and remaining porcelain.

For Franck, Evelyne and the museum personnel there was still at least a year's work to do. Everything had to be correlated against the computerized catalogue prepared during excavation, the porcelain needed detailed inspection, restoration and classification by design, type and purpose, and samples had to be sent to Europe for analysis. There were also exhibitions to organize, photography and drawings to be arranged, methods of preservation to be discussed and decided upon, and the technical report to be written once all the results had come in.

For Kris, too, the work had only just begun. He returned to England and went back to the records, searching for more clues, and worked on models to try and reproduce what had happened to the ship. There was also the film which he, Lenora Carey and Mark Balsiger had shot and the editing, scripting and production of this was six months' work alone. Kris needed to talk to experts in a multitude of fields and found that the volume of specialized knowledge was in fact tiny and mainly conjectural as so few wrecks of this period have been discovered. Shipwrecks and what happens once a vessel is under water continue to remain a mystery and that is one of the reasons why their study will always attract people. There were also museums to consult over matching types and designs of porcelain, and much consideration was given as to the best way of publicizing the *Griffin* and displaying the discoveries. Every effort was made to keep the operation secret as he did not want to do anything until after everything had been properly studied and we were especially wary of the possibility of someone else going to the site and destroying what was there with large scale equipment in a careless and greedy smash-and-grab operation.

In the wake of the phenomenal success of Michael Hatcher's *Geldermalsen* porcelain, in the 'Nanking Sale' at Christie's in Amsterdam in April 1986, we knew that the *Griffin*'s cargo was worth a fortune. In London in late 1986 even the most ordinary bowls from the *Geldermalsen*, which had been destined for Cape Town and did not even qualify as export porcelain, were fetching over £100 despite the fact that there were tens of thousands of them. The quality pieces went for thousands of pounds. The *Griffin*'s cargo was all high quality and the smaller amount, combined with the fact that it was intended for an English market and came from the only English ship which will probably ever be found with porcelain on board, meant that we could have been looking at several million pounds. With our requests to look through old sale catalogues to match designs, it did not take long for several auction houses and large shops to hear about what we had found and wonderful offers and elaborate concepts were put forward for marketing the find, but the *Griffin* was not for sale. Kris wants the collection to remain complete and to be exhibited from time to time. He is prepared to lend part of it to any *bona fide* display but, above all, is determined that the *Griffin*'s relics, unlike so many others of the East India Company, will not be buried in a museum store to be brought out every ten years or so for an occasional showing. We hope that one day a museum to the Company will be established and that the *Griffin*'s cargo will find a home within it.

Back in Manila the house we had rented was filled with thousands and thousands of plates, bowls, mugs and cups, all in individual plastic bags each bearing its own computerized access number. They had been soaked in fresh water on board the *China Sea Explorer* to remove much of the salt before it dried and were now processed through a number of baths full of distilled water. This gave the conservators their first real opportunity for classification. The pieces were first separated into groups according to their shape: cups for tea, coffee and chocolate, saucers, small and large plates, platters, bowls, tea and coffee pots, lids, caddies, jugs, beer mugs and everything else. Then the blue and white pieces were separated from the enamelled ones, and finally matching designs were made up into services. The *blanc de chine* figures and unique pieces were kept separate for the time being.

Chinese porcelain was manufactured in two major places: Jingdezhen (Ching-tê Chên) in Kiangsi province, about 600 miles north of Canton, is where the blue and white originates, whilst the more unusual *blanc de chine* came from Dehua (Tê-hua) in southern China's Fukien province. The vast majority, however, came from Jingdezhen and was taken by inland rivers and canals to the port of Nanking (hence the popular term for Chinese porcelain 'Nanking ware') and from there shipped to Canton and other places. The Chinese were loath to give Europeans any glimpse of their country and absolutely forbade travel outside the ports to all save missionaries. Fortunately one of these, Father d'Entrecolles, went to Jingdezhen and was able to publish a description in 1738, in which he said that the village (so called because it lacked a city wall) had a population of one million and was built along a four-mile stretch of a beautiful river. He went on to say that there were more than 500 furnaces and the best workmen in porcelain worked in hundreds, if not thousands, of small studios.

In the thirteenth century the Venetians and other great city states sent merchants like Marco Polo to China and they brought back some of the earliest porcelain, but in more modern times the first shipments of any quantity were made by the Portuguese during the sixteenth century. It was an immediate success and much sought after, more for its curiosity value than anything else. The new product was in demand all over Europe and the Portuguese kept their monopoly until the Dutch and then the English began to import it by way of Batavia and India from about 1660. If people did not use pewter or silver tableware, the alternative at this time was earthenware with a tin-based white glaze applied on top, which was brittle, chipped off easily and was basically unsatisfactory. The Company imported porcelain from 1687 and it became an important part of every cargo after 1700, when the first ship traded successfully in Canton. Father d'Entrecolles also gave details of the raw materials and methods employed by the Chinese, which gave a boost to the European potteries, but it was not until the late eighteenth century that they could begin to compete with the Chinese product and then only after an import duty of over 100% had been imposed, so for most of the 1700s the Company's chinaware was in a class of its own.

The potters of Jingdezhen were fortunate in that their 'village' was situated near huge deposits of white clay, rich in the vitally important component felspar from the eroded granite mountains which surrounded them. This was mined in large quantities and distributed amongst the hundreds of small workshops, where the potters would sit on the ground with their legs stretched out around their wheels and turn a plate or cup, unlike the Europeans, whose porcelain is much less pliable and could only be shaped from moulds. The potters then left the piece to dry before it was delivered in a fragile state to a painter for decorating with a cobalt based pigment. This also differed from the Europeans', as they would have fired the piece before the design was applied, but the kilns of Jingdezhen were some distance from the potters' establishments and the single firing probably evolved as a method of saving time. Once they had finished work, the painters dipped the product into a vat of glaze and this was again left to dry before being put back on to the wheel to have any drips of glaze taken off. Then a number of pieces were placed on a type of tray or board and carried on the shoulder through the crowded streets to the kiln. Before being fired the plate is opaque and porous, the decoration appears black and the glaze is the colour of chalk. During firing at 1,350° to 1,450°C. the cobalt in the paint turns blue and actually fuses with the glaze, so what is usually called underglaze porcelain is in fact inglaze. Both the glaze and the porcelain are hardened and vitrified by such great heat and the finished product, if less than 5 mm thick, is translucent, if tapped lightly has a ring to it and has many of the characteristics of glass. Export porcelain, due to its enormous quantity, tends, on the whole, to be thicker.

To some pieces extra decoration in colours ranging from red to green and yellow was added. This was applied over the glaze and then fired again at a lower temperature. This enamelling was done almost solely in Canton to European orders. The Chinese had experimented with overglaze colouring for several centuries, but it was not until the Jesuits began to teach copper enamelling and the supracargoes asked, in 1710, if their own designs could be made that the Chinese realized they could make a market out of what they termed 'foreign colours'. These became the most desirable porcelains and, whilst the Company was sending instructions for the purchase of useful sorts, private individuals who knew captains or other officers would place orders with them for special patterns, often incorporating their coat of arms or initials, in enamel. Sometimes instructions were written at the edge of the artwork and these too were faithfully copied by the Chinese painters much to the annoyance of their owners. Special orders became so popular that potters in Jingdezhen were even asked to supply completely undecorated blanks for later enamelling in Canton. The styles became known according to their major colours, *famille verte* was predominantly green and *famille rose* mainly red. Some examples also copied the Japaneses Imari pattern of adding a gilding to the design and from time to time pieces are seen with European pictures reproduced from engravings or portraits of East Indiamen.

By the early part of the eighteenth century the taste in England had shifted dramatically towards China. Everything from long case clocks to chests of drawers were lacquered and painted with pseudo Chinese scenes. The Europeanized porcelain designs were a great success and by 1720 the Company was sending instructions to the supracargoes to order chinaware a year in advance to ensure good quality and delivery. By the 1740s enamelled ware had become so popular that simple blue and white tea services were quite rare. The supracargoes were also told to ask for special shapes and from about 1760 until the trade ceased in 1791 only four designs were used at any one time, these being changed infrequently, so that replacements for broken pieces were more easily available.

We were fortunate in that it was immediately clear that the *Griffin*'s porcelain had many more than four patterns, so the Company's directives had not been received in 1758–59, when the order for the 1760 ships was made. What was apparent, however, was that the European shapes had been requested, as we found blue and white tea services with three differently shaped rims and a number of octagonal pieces. The principal designs we found included one with exotic fruit including the pineapple, which was a popular symbol in England, two renditions of the famous water and temple scene, several different arrangements featuring trees, and a number of flowers. There were numerous borders ranging from simple lines to complicated geometric designs and one important and rare set featured a four-part wave pattern with a crane in the centre and was a copy of Japanese porcelain.

Most of the *Griffin*'s chinaware was blue and white inglaze which had additionally been enamelled. Unfortunately, because all the chests had broken open, the plates lying by themselves were exposed to the destructive elements in the water and nearly all traces of enamel have disappeared. As a result of this, comparative studies with perfectly preserved pieces in museums and collections around the world were necessary and most of the missing designs have now been traced. Many of our plates are, in effect, identical to the blanks which were shipped from Jingdezhen to Canton. Some of the pieces, especially beer mugs, are completely white but under certain light it is possible to see where the enamel had been applied and even to make out the original patterns.

The supracargoes in Canton are on record as packing their porcelain in sago for shipment back to England. We found a number of cups and bowls which were still stacked inside each other as they had originally been and inside these were traces of vegetable material, which has been analysed. Our findings have established that tea and rice as well as sago were used in the packing process and, where these have not been swept away by the water, more enamels are preserved. Enamels were also protected when plates had been covered by calcerous marine growths, barnacles or algae, but in all cases what was left had turned black. Even when used normally these overglaze decorations were always susceptible to chipping, flaking and general fading through cleaning, and perfect pieces are seldom seen, so it was hardly surprising that enamels which had been under water for over 200 years had disappeared. It is actually rather astonishing that any were left and the preservation of these and the restoration of original colours taxed Evelyne's knowledge considerably. Eventually she hit upon the idea of treating them with an oxidizing chemical, acting on the premise that, as the original colours were composed of alkaline or neutral oxides, the acidic bacteria which had altered them could be removed with this. Hydrogen peroxide (H_2O_2) was used and worked brilliantly with red iron oxide based paints, restoring the original colour in a matter of seconds. The other colours took longer to appear and she was never able to bring back their full pigment. Perhaps future chemical research will unearth something to bring back the greens and yellows but, for the time being, all the enamels that we have revived are coated with a thin acrylic resin to protect them.

Probably the most exciting discovery in the category of blue and white and enamelled ware was the almost complete case of crab and prawn octagonal plates. The Company had first sent out requests for this shape in 1755, so they were still quite an innovation at the time the *Griffin* sank and, as importation ceased in 1785, it is not a common shape. On one of the loose plates which had fallen out of the missing corner of the chest (there were about twenty of these all stacked together lying nearby) we found some enamel traces and were able to match it to one in perfect condition in store at the British Museum, the only other one in existence so far as we know. At present the fate of this chest is undecided; it would be fascinating to look at the plates which are still packed together to see if any enamels on these have been saved, but, on the other hand, a complete chest of this type is an extraordinary subject in itself.

Another interesting design is that known as the fish roe diaper. A number of pieces from tea services of this were found in the centre of the *Griffin*'s hull, underneath and near the large lumps of coral. It is a well-documented pattern and must have been available in the enamelling shops of Canton for several years as a teapot c.1765 is known decorated with Lord Clive's coat of arms and several other pieces have been traced with various other designs. We found some of this pattern with enough enamel intact to be able to make out the subject, which is an amusing one, showing two ladies looking at bowls while three boys play around a table and a dog looks on. It seems to depict a scene inside a china shop and a similar pattern was found on a teapot stand in a private collection in Paris. It has a different blue and white pattern, so does not come from the same series as the ones we have, but this proves that it must have been a standard design at least in 1760. Almost all Chinese export porcelain is of the hard paste variety, but in recent years several studies have been published showing that some is what is known as soft paste or of a more grainy texture, and many of the pieces in this set fall into this rather unusual category.

There was some confusion and much discussion over the composition of the tea services we found. One book on the French East India Company states that a standard tea service consisted of twelve cups and saucers, one tea canister (caddy), one tea pot, one sugar bowl and one compôte, whilst it seems that the usual English tea set comprised forty-three pieces: teapot, cover and stand, sugar bowl, cover and plate, slop bowl and plate, tea canister and cover, milk pot and cover, spoon tray, twelve tea bowls and saucers, and six coffee cups. Complete sets like this are unusual and we did not find any on the *Griffin*, although the presence of milk jugs, lids and slop bowls confirms that there were some. We formed the conclusion that, because of the huge number of cups and saucers, many people used silver tea pots, jugs and sugar bowls in preference to porcelain ones, as they still do, and merely purchased what they wanted. This is borne out by the auction lists of the period and a painting in the Victoria and Albert Museum c.1740–50 showing a typical family group taking tea with Chinese porcelain cups and saucers whilst everything else is silver. Those who could afford porcelain in the mid-eighteenth century could also buy silver and many seemed to have preferred to do so.

The list of porcelain purchases recorded in the China factory diary in 1759 almost certainly includes consignments for the *Griffin* and shows, in 100 chests, only 91 tea sets and 21,110 pairs of cups and saucers with 16,275 single plates. There are two different patterns of tea set and we found four, the Japanese one and a beautiful sprig design set were probably part of the private trade. Of the two which we believe were the Company's order, one, described in the diary as enamelled, is the fish roe diaper design and the other emerged devoid of all enamels and completely white. The diary described this set as bone, so possibly it was never enamelled in the first place, but this would be extremely rare and requires further investigation. There are entries for five types of cups and saucers, and six designs of single plates. Most of the cups and saucers are enamelled, only 4,326 are not, but curiously only 7,101 single plates are not blue and white. It had seemed likely that these would be in designs matching the cups and saucers, but the *Griffin*'s cargo confirmed that this was not the case in any instance. It appears that, in 1761, if a purchaser wanted matching plates for his cups and saucers, he would have to buy a whole tea service. There are twenty-two main patterns of tea cups or bowls, one of the most unusual featured a crane holding a fish in its beak; the others were the more common scenes of trees and riverscapes with houses or temples and arrangements of flowers. The 'Japanese set' was the only one where we found two-handled coffee cups in a service, but there were a number of single coffee cups which had been enamelled. Most of these have ended up pure white, but a few still have traces of the design, which is a riverscape with a bridge and overhanging blossom tree. The sprig service did not have any two handled cups, but did have some with a single handle and whether this was a variation or if these were for chocolate we are not sure. The tea bowls tend to have a diameter across the rim of just under 8 cm and are $3\frac{1}{2}$ cm high with saucers varying between 11 and $12\frac{1}{2}$ cm. Some have borders around the rims and most have a single flower at the bottom of the inside. The coffee cups are thinner and taller as they often are today, and the better quality sets, which we think are most likely private trade, tend to be slightly larger.

We also found a number of chocolate cups and beer mugs in three different sizes. Once again these could be confirmed from the diary with entries stating '80 sets of 3 mugs' and '1,071 cups with handles'.

The chocolate cups were painted completely with a house, tree and mountains in the background, matching in many ways a drawing of the mountains surrounding Jingdezhen. Even though there was only one pattern on a large quantity of these, it was fascinating to see how many small variations there are as different hands painted the same scene. Our experiences with most of the other sets was that there were hardly any changes whatsoever and this led to the conclusion that these must have been painted by one person working from a pattern. Of the beer mugs we found several different shapes and designs, and all came in quarter, half and whole pint measures. Most had been enamelled and the places where this had been applied were obvious by differently shaped cartouches and lozenges on the main body. Most had a single blue border just under the lip and another around the base. Only one with all blue decoration was found and this was unfortunately in fragments which have now been pieced together to show an intricate pattern of a fence or balcony with numerous flowers, bamboo plants and rocks.

This is the full extent of the pieces which could be matched to the official cargo belonging to the Company according to the records in the China factory diary. Everything else must have belonged to the private trade and included in this was a fortunate find of a stack of twenty-four large platters or meat dishes. There are four different designs and two shapes, oval and octagonal. Two designs show flowers, one a water scene with boatmen and the other is a landscape with a pierced trellis and deer. Each piece is blue and white, in excellent condition and we are able to match one to a collection of dinner plates, so it must have belonged to a complete service. The diary, in years before the *Griffin*, had given details of what these comprised: dishes, plates, side dishes, soup plates, salad dishes, sauce boats, salts and tureens with lids and stands. We did not find any blue and white tureens and only one hexagonal enamelled example which came with its lid and matches three bowls, but the deeper of the platters are probably stands for these. There are, however, quantities of everything else which make up a dinner service or 'table set' as the supracargoes called them, including two differently shaped salts. Altogether, we had representative pieces from seven or eight sets, some of which were blue and white and others partially or completely enamelled. The records show that the Company's services could contain anything from 40 to 118 pieces and certainly some private commissions were much larger with as many as 300 or more pieces.

In addition to these private trade items we found sets of punch bowls, covered jars, beakers, three types of mantle garniture, four types of enamelled stands and several large covered vases. There was also a smattering of figures and *blanc de chine*. Unlike everything else, these came from Dehua in southern China, which was renowned for producing hand-made figures of superb quality and glaze. *Blanc de chine* figures are undecorated and usually take the form of Buddhist gods or Taoist immortals. We found examples of both including a large one 52 cm high. These, together with animals, had been common in Amoy and were regularly brought back when ships used this port. After foreign traders were confined to Canton, they still appeared and were popular for a century, rarely changing in design. Michael Hatcher found *blanc de chine* on the *Geldermalsen* and his examples are almost identical to those of the *Griffin* except that ours have different bases, the figures standing on clouds rather than rectangular plinths. We did not find many animal figures other than two types of dogs. These were either lying down or sitting up and had been enamelled red with contrasting collars in Canton.

Private trade also traditionally included Chinese products which did not interest the Company. In early records are noted shipments of mother-of-pearl tables, umbrellas, gold and, most often, fans. We found parts of a number of high-quality ivory fans which could be joined together by a pivoting pin at the bottom in groups of four to make anything from a very small to very large fan. The way these fans were put together is that the main sail or mount can be made of anything from silk to paper and this is stitched on to a stick, which is the ivory part we found. When the fan is folded up, each side had a guard, which is solid, but the sticks are finely carved with four-part central scenes and much delicately carved geometric tracery, and a rib extending up to which the mount is sewn. The mounts were attached both in China and England, and in the Victoria and Albert Museum is a fan almost identical to the pieces we found with a mount which appears to be English, leading to the conclusion that the ones we found were packed loose and made up later.

It is a sad fact that the current swept away almost all artefacts relating to the crew. Those who found the *Amsterdam* were terribly fortunate in that her hull had been buried in the beach and was full of sand. They found a large quantity of personal articles ranging from shoe leathers to buttons, combs, belts and cutlery. Similar things were also found on the wreck of HMS *Invincible* (1757), which also sank in English waters, but we were not so lucky. We did find several shoe buckles which certainly belonged to officers, as the discoveries on the other ships had established that sailors wore shoes with fold-over leather uppers. One of these buckles retains some original gilding and all are of European origin. We found some things which we had not expected, including these buckles, as we had thought most shoes would have worn out by the time the ship left China and would have been replaced locally. If this was the case, then buckles were retained and re-used, but we did not know how many pairs of shoes a man would take on an eighteen-month voyage and perhaps they did not use Chinese cobblers at all.

Clay tobacco pipes make a fascinating study and we found several which are of interest to specialists in this field. They were originally purchased complete with tobacco and were designed to be thrown away after being smoked, which is why they occur in virtually all archaeological sites after about 1600. We knew from the *Amsterdam's* wreck, where a complete box of unsmoked examples was found, that they formed a normal part of a ship's supplies, but, as the *Griffin* had been away from England for so long, we did not expect to find any on her. On 24 March 1759, just before she left the Thames, a note in the log informs us that eight casks of tobacco were loaded on board, but whether this was loose leaf intended for India or pipes for the crew is not clear. If this was the crew's ration, it seems to be a small quantity for 100 men and we thought that, by the time the ship arrived in Canton, they would have finished them and changed over to the long Chinese pipes, but of these we found no sign.

Close inspection of the pipes in Manila revealed two sets of makers' marks. One, the initials wm within a circle, refers to William Manbey, who was active in London between 1750 and 1770. He seems to have catered almost solely for ships, as identical examples have been found at Port Royal in Jamaica and in Williamsburg and Louisburg in America, whilst only one has been found in England. The other pipe presents an interesting puzzle. Its mark is that of three crowns with the initials fr underneath, and similar specimens have been found both in London and Sweden. The London examples also have the initials wm and one expert believes that William Manbey made these pipes to celebrate King Frederick the Great of Prussia, who was England's ally during the Seven Years War, 1756–63. Commemorative examples such as this were quite common and would have been on sale together with the maker's standard pipes.

It stands to reason that this pipemaker supplied the *Griffin* with all the pipes on board, except for one curious fact. When the *Griffin* arrived at Whampoa on 15 July 1760, her log noted: 'was saluted by the *Valentine*, Captain Fernell with 7 guns and by the Swede ship with 9 guns'. The cypher on the second pipe is identical to that of

Frederick, King of Sweden, and pipes with this mark have been attributed to factories in Varberg and Stockholm. The Swedish ship in Whampoa had wintered over, having missed the monsoon, so if the *Griffin*'s sailors purchased pipes from her, she must have had a great number on board to be able to spare some. On the other hand, what was William Manbey doing making pipes with the King of Sweden's insignia on when that country had prohibited their importation since 1749? Irregularities such as this, exposing gaps in our knowledge, is what makes archaeology fascinating. Unfortunately, we have not been able to confirm whether the Swedish ship had pipes for sale, but the FR attribution to Sweden, rather than Prussia, seems more reasonable. The pipes found in London with the Swedish mark have all been discovered along the City foreshore, so perhaps William Manbey was making pipes and supplying them to Swedish sailors, thereby circumventing the ban on imports. If a Swedish ship had not been at Whampoa, this would have been the explanation, but, until more information comes to light, the origin of the *Griffin*'s pipes remains an enigma.

There are numerous contemporary accounts of officers carrying wine with them and the *Griffin* was no exception as her log records that, on 9 April 1759, the Captain was delivered of seventeen casks. Two days later he received five cases of glasses and ten hampers of wine, and the other officers also brought varying quantities on board. Most Indiamen called in at Madeira or one of its neighbouring islands on the outward voyage and bought large supplies of wine, both for personal consumption and for sale in India, but the *Griffin* was unusual in that she never stopped there and must have relied on what she had loaded in England. We found several wine bottles in four different shapes, one has a tall square body, another is round with a long body and neck similar to a modern bottle, and two are squat with short necks. All these types were in common use in England in 1759 and each shape was intended for a different drink, port, brandy or French red. The cask and hampers which were loaded on board referred to two different sizes of barrel, as wine was not sold bottled and the captain's steward would decant it before each meal. Of the five cases of wine glasses, these had all disappeared with the exception of one broken stem. This was, again, typical of the mid-eighteenth century, long and containing a spiral of white enamel decoration incorporated into the glass.

In addition to the iron ballast bars we also uncovered several adzes and other tools, a quantity of lead shot and numerous cannon balls, in three sizes, but no cannons or any furniture from ships chests and barrels. This was not wholly unexpected as we were sure that everything readily movable had been thrown overboard to lighten the ship and would have either sunk near the reef or been carried away by the current as the *Pocock*'s officer had reported. The close proximity of the NPA base on Kaludud prevented a really detailed study of the reef, but the cannons, had they been there, would surely have shown up on the survey. At this stage it seemed most likely that the fishermen salvaged and sold them shortly after the wreck.

The theory that the hull, or at least the front section of it, was still partially intact when the ship stopped in its present position is supported by the discovery of three iron kettles amongst the timbers which probably came from the cook-house in the fo'c'sle and were swept downwards when the surrounding timbers began to break up. They were standard items in England during the eighteenth century and could be placed on hot plates, suspended above a fire on a bracket called a cranes chimney, or kept on small stands with a candle or burner beneath. These do not appear anywhere on the *Griffin*'s lists, which is hardly surprising as things like this were part of the essential equipment, but it is interesting to note that, when the *Griffin* was in Bombay, a number of kettles exactly matching these were loaded on board to be delivered to the troops stationed at Tellicherry. Did some get misplaced?

Our small collection of objects and artefacts all have English origins and did not tell us anything about whether the sailors mixed and shopped at Whampoa as we had hoped they might. Sailors only went to Canton when rowing an officer up river and never stayed there long, but Whampoa had its own small town and it would have been interesting to find the sort of everyday Chinese things which would confirm that the shops sold goods apart from alcohol. Before leaving the Thames, each man received two months advance wages, so he had a little money to spend but, as the ship provided everything he wanted, perhaps he had no need, no desire or no opportunity to go out and replace worn out articles of clothing and buy souvenirs. Unfortunately, the *Griffin*'s wreck does not provide the answer, as the only Chinese item we found was one coin of the smallest denomination, 'cash'. This was worth one-thousandth of a tael, or less than one-tenth of a penny, so may have been the small change after a days' drinking or a memento from China to take home when nothing else was available.

Inspecting the hull was an entirely different matter to making conjectures about life in Whampoa and examining the porcelain. Most fortuitously we knew that the *Griffin* had been built in Perry's Yard at Blackwell on the River Thames. At exactly the same time as her keel was laid that of another Indiaman, the *Boscawen*, was also begun and her original specification survives among the papers of her owner, Samuel Braund, in the Essex County Records Office so it can be confidently assumed that the two were virtually identical.

In several English museums, especially the Science Museum in London, are to be found original shipwrights' working models showing the skeleton and construction of men-of-war, but nowhere in England are any similar models of mid-eighteenth century East Indiamen and the complete example in the National Maritime Museum of the *Somerset* (1738) is far too valuable to pull apart to see if the interior details are as accurate as the exterior ones. The hull of the *Griffin*, therefore, gave us a unique opportunity to examine the construction of an East Indiaman at its most vulnerable and important stage. Contemporary records explain the procedures and the *Boscawen* contract provided exact dimensions of the timbers and major bolts, so we were able to start with the keel itself and work through each stage of building a ship to see if the details in the *Boscawen* specification were copied for the *Griffin*.

The Perry Yard stated that the keel was 105′ long and 14″ square. The *Griffin*'s was 96′6″ and, in its decomposing state, near enough to 14″ to confirm this. As no oak tree grows straight for such a long way, we discovered that the *Griffin*'s keel was made up of three pieces and had snapped at the join of a fourth. These joins were hollowed out or rebated to allow the next piece, which had a long tongue, to fit in snugly and were secured with four long drawn bolts. After this was completed, the shipwright then turned to the framing or ribs, which would give the sides their shape. Each of these ribs was made from several pieces shaped as the curve of the sides required, but the bottom of an East Indiaman was flat for a greater distance than is the case with a man-of-war because these ships were designed to be wide with large holds. The bottom framing timbers or futtocks of the *Griffin* run continuously from side to side and are bolted to the keel from underneath with a gap of 12″ to 14″ between each one. Once this was done, another long piece, identical to the keel, known as the keelson was placed on top and bolts were placed downwards into the futtocks giving extra strength. The futtocks, like the keel, are massive pieces of wood, each measuring about 12″ × 9″ and in the centre section of the hull, where the ship would have been at its broadest, there are twenty-five of these each about 22′ long. They had all broken where the next piece would have been joined on to begin the curve of the sides. Several still had their bolts in place, but the majority had been ripped out, leaving a jagged edge, probably when the ship rolled over on the bottom.

The voids between each futtock were filled with other timbers of a similar size, which have been bolted on to the keel (rather than on top) and given a slight angle, so that by the time they reached the beginning of the upwards curve of the ship's sides, they were level. These were then covered with more pieces which were pegged into place using wooden dowels called treenails. It is widely assumed that these were made from fine grained and therefore stronger pieces of oak from the top of the tree, but our analysis of one proved that it was actually rosewood from South America, which was something of a surprise as the only wood from this area being brought regularly to England in 1748 was mahogany. All the other timbers were oak grown in the south of England with the exception of some pulleys and blocks which were elm with *lignum vitae* pins.

The keelson was 8″ shorter at the bow than the keel and we could only explain this by thinking that there must have been a corner block attached between it and the stem post which rose up to make the bow shape. It was 20 m or $66\frac{2}{3}'$ long and was also made from several pieces and had, like the keel, broken away at a join towards the stern. The joins in these two long pieces were staggered for extra strength and, when the keelson came away, this caused all the nearest pieces filling the gaps between the futtocks to come adrift, which had in turn weakened the flooring timbers running parallel to the keelson. This was the reason for the break up of the stern, which is constructed around a piece joined in at nearly right angles to the keel called the stern post. From this came out a number of very heavy pieces called transoms, which embrace the sides of the ship and form the frame of the entire rear part of the vessel. At some stage the ship had been smashed down and this had caused the keel, keelson and stern post to break upwards which would have made the transoms part from the futtocks and pulled off the timbers on the sides. The *Griffin* literally broke her back. If this happened on the reef it would have hastened the sinking and perhaps the stern came away and lies further north than the hull, but until it is found no one can say. Unfortunately the model we constructed could not be subjected to the same conditions as the *Griffin* experienced because the exact circumstances are not known and, in tests, the model did not behave in the same way as a ship would have done.

The flooring timbers, which were bolted on to the futtocks, were described in the Perry specification as being 12″ × 13″. We found that, although some were 12″ wide, many were much narrower, no more than 8″ thick. The greatest concentration of them was found on the left side of the hull, where eight are still in place, covering an area of about 275 square feet. On the right up to seven rows are still fixed and these cover about 180 square feet. The longest timber is 26′, but most are exactly 20′ and all are oak.

The timbers which were exposed to the water, the outboard planking, are fixed to the futtocks with bolts and run parallel with the keel. They are mainly covered with a further layer of boards, which was especially necessary in vessels that sailed in warmer waters to inhibit the teredo worm and prolong the ship's life. Each of the shipyards which built Indiamen had a different technique for protecting their ships against these worms and the Perry specification said: 'To sheathe the bottom with good three-quarter inch board; to fire and tar the parcelling and to nail it on. To cant the wales [thicker pieces on the ship's side] as usual and to paint the bottom with white stuff and find spunyard [old cordage, etc., used to fill up gaps] and nails.' Most other yards used a mixture of hair and tar, and the Perrys have been stated to have used tarred paper, but parcelling is a type of heavy duty canvas and this is exactly what we found, covered with thick tar which was still in remarkably good watertight, and presumably worm-proof, condition. All of the nails had rusted away, but stained holes where they had been could still be made out.

Our examination of the hull showed up the weak points of a ship. As was to be expected, these were where the ribs had been joined together at the base of the upwards curve and the joins in the keel for the stem and stern posts. It was somewhat surprising that the keel and keelson had also broken away, for these two pieces, together with the futtocks which cross them, are 3′ thick. Had these timbers not been broken, the hull would probably have stayed together for much longer. Once the stern section had been loosened, the disintegration of the sides was a matter of course.

It would be nice to think that one day a more complete East Indiaman of the *Griffin*'s type might be found. There are several possibilities and we are considering the *Denham*, which was set on fire and scuttled whilst in port in Sumatra to avoid capture by the French. If her hull was not too badly damaged under the waterline and sank in shallow muddy water, she may still be in fair condition, but the expense of an operation such as ours is prohibitive if nothing of value is salvaged and most Governments do not have the resources or the interest to fund such a salvage. In the meantime, until another

CHAPTER 8

The Riddle of the Griffin

Thomas Dethick was glad as he stepped into the passage boat which was taking him down to Whampoa two to three hours row away. It was not that the factory was uncomfortable, nor the other captains and supracargoes bad company, he was just tired of Canton. Canton, the great city heaving with all forms of humanity, most of it low in his estimation, where one could never walk alone for fear of being attacked or crowded in by a group of youths and finding one's pockets empty once they dispersed. From previous experience he knew never to take his watch and chain, and this was infuriating as the Chinese did not seem to have any idea of the time; what happened to the clocks he sold to the *hongists* was a mystery. He found the continual cries of, '*Fan kwae, Fan kwae,*' (foreign devil) which rang out behind him or were whispered from darkened rooms as he passed on his way to the chinaware dealers irritating and this was one of several aspects of China with which he had never come to terms. Earlier that morning, as he stood on the balcony watching the thousands of boats which had in the past held him mesmerized for hours, he had calculated that today, 30 December, was the 168th day of his stay in Canton – five and a half months – and now he was leaving for home.

The first two months were always busy with ordering the china-ware, but this had gone down to the *Griffin* on 9 October. Since then he had bought some tea, always a good insurance in case the home-ward voyage was rough and the china smashed; gone to the Fa-tee gardens, a couple of miles up river; and competed with all the other captains for the few figures and statues which were occasionally avail-able in the Amoy china shop. These were in short supply this year, which was disappointing as they always sold well and it was also unfortunate that no one at home had given him an order for a painted dinner service, the processing of which would have occupied a couple of weeks. Other than taking the eighteen-mile walk around the city walls, these were almost the only diversions available in Canton.

The last shipment of tea, together with his box of ivory fans, had left on the 22nd. Eight days gave the crew plenty of time to finish stowing everything and he had received a note from Charles Hudson two days previously saying all was ready. Mr Lockwood and Mr Wood, the supracargoes, had occupied themselves with clearing the factory and placing orders for next year whilst waiting for the grand chop, which the merchant Chetqua had finally delivered the previous evening. This meant that the ships were allowed to depart, leaving Mr Wood to finish the last small details before heading down to Macau, where he would wait until next season's ships arrived. Mr Lockwood was, of course, going home on the *Griffin*.

Dinner, served by stony-faced Chinese servants, began slightly earlier than usual and was finished by 2 p.m., when Chetqua's passage boat was due to arrive. This was a lovely roomy affair, more like a floating house, with several chambers, beautiful carvings, pictures and the windows were glazed, unlike the mother-of-pearl which was installed in most Chinese houses. Once underway, Thomas Dethick looked out and watched as the city was gradually replaced by a more rural aspect and he waited to see the lotus flower enclosures, now sadly all dead and brown, a complete change from the blaze of colour which had greeted his arrival in July.

His thoughts were interrupted by a question from William Webber, commander of the *Oxford*. He knew young William's father, who was also a captain and had been in China when the *Griffin* made her second call in 1753, and now he was asking what everyone thought of Mr Dalrymple leading them back through the Philippines. This was a vexatious matter as far as Thomas Dethick was concerned. He had not formed a favourable opinion of the brash young man who had come up to Canton in November full of stories of Portuguese 'insults to the British nation' and how he would write to the Secretary of State and insist that the King learned of his troubles. Dethick was far too experienced and pragmatic to be concerned with all Dalrymple's pretensions and had been amazed when told that he and his snow, the *Cuddalore*, had been moored at Macau and Whampoa almost continually for eighteen months; he wondered what Dalrymple had been doing all that time.

There was, however, the serious problem of two French men-of-war which had been reported cruising somewhere off the coast of Sumatra, all ready to capture the slow, heavily laden English ships as they passed through, so when Dalrymple had finally confided the true nature of his secret mission to Thomas Lockwood and assured him of his possession of Spanish sailing directions for the Philippines, it was with some relief that the supracargo was able officially to request the *Cuddalore* to guide the Indiamen to the Macassar Strait, thereby taking them well away from where the French ships would be lying in wait. This was a double coup for Mr Lockwood as the Chinese had grown upset and suspicious over why the *Cuddalore* was refusing to pay measurage and ordered her out. Now the supra-cargoes could be seen to be complying with this and were able to justify the expense of re-provisioning her, which, up to now, she having nothing to do with trade, had been outside their jurisdiction.

Finally the Whampoa pagoda came into view and, as they passed the island, the ships were seen in the middle of the river looking very fine, newly painted and with pennants flying from all masts. The boat called to the *Griffin* before any other and, as she came along-side, the gunner sounded first one salute for the captain and then another for Mr Lockwood. Acrid blue smoke enveloped the ship, but there was no mistaking the commodore's flag at her masthead or the welcome on board, and Thomas Dethick felt proud. It was a pleasure to see the old ship looking so good with her rigging freshly tarred and brasswork gleaming, but the decks looked a trifle messy with goats and cows tethered to the main-mast, piles of straw all along the waistboards between the gun carriages and a stack of coops on the poop, from which issued a terrible chorus of squawking and hooting. Charles Hudson stepped forward first as befitted his position as chief mate. Behind him stood the other officers, Dr Herriot, the second passenger, and Mr Lockwood's servant, gesticulating to his master. The two of them disappeared down towards the great cabin, obviously to sort out some of the vast quantity of his goods which now filled the space, and Captain Dethick, in his official voice, enquired, 'All well, Mr Hudson?' Upon receiving the expected affirm-ative reply, he ushered his friend through the doors and into the round house for a more informal conversation about the lading, the crew and the ship's condition.

Later, all the captains came to the *Griffin* for supper and to hear Mr Dalrymple give his explanation as to the course they would steer. The packet of the Company's instructions for returning ships was also opened, the older captains taking little notice of the exhortations to protect the Company's investment, the younger ones avidly read-ing everything. There was nothing new, they would sail direct to St Helena and, should intelligence be received there of a war, wait for an escort or, should one not be expected, sail in line directly to England without stopping at Ascension and make every effort to avoid any sail, lest she be an enemy.

At 6 a.m. the following morning the ship weighed anchor and came about to face the sea. All the others copied her and by 9 a.m. they were under way, having waited to ensure that high tide would coincide with their passing over the sandbanks in the river. Thomas Dethick, on his poop deck, saw the landing site on Danes Island pass by and caught a glimpse of French Island, where, five months earlier, he had buried his servant of eight years, Thomas Godfrey. This had been his third voyage on the *Griffin*, no other captain he knew had had such a devoted man, and telling his wife was not a task Thomas Dethick looked forward to, especially as she was also employed in his house.

The ship passed over the first and second bars and, leaving the Bocca Tigris, entered the Bogue just after noon. Macau was now only a few hours' sail and the ships, sailing in line, kept to the middle to avoid coming too close to the many islands and sheltered bays, all known to be infested with pirates. By late afternoon it was turning colder and the chance of a sea mist made the fleet drop anchor for the night in a sheltered bay at Lintin Island. Next morning, New Year's Day 1761, at 6 a.m. the anchors were raised and the ships were soon under way, aiming to pass to the south-west of the Grand Ladrone, which they duly did in the early hours of the next day. It was now all open sea to the Spanish island of Luconia (Luzon).

This sail was not nearly so easy as cruising with the monsoon down the Chinese Sea. Almost immediately the ships ran into a head swell and strong winds made them toss and turn. Two days out the *Griffin*'s top sail split and slowed progress through the heaving water even further. Thomas Dethick ordered a good lookout every night in case the coast came up sooner than he imagined and made certain all the hatches were well battened down for fear the sea would begin to break over the ship. By the 7th the weather had still not moderated and the officers were keen to run in fast for the land, but could not, owing to the fact that the *Suffolk* had proved to be a slug and was miles behind them. The coastline was finally seen at daybreak on 9 January, and thankfully the wind and sea eased up as the day progressed. Soundings revealed no ground, which was a relief, but the captain was taking no chances and turned his ship to the south when she was still twenty miles from land.

A couple of days later they had their first sighting of the *Cuddalore* since leaving the Pearl River. Dethick had, by this time, made his way past Manila Point and now, in his capacity as the fleet's commodore, asked Dalrymple to ensure that the *Cuddalore* guide the Indiamen properly through all the straits ahead. The *Suffolk* was still lagging a long way behind and, almost as if to be annoying, Dalrymple sailed with her for the next two days. Fortunately, the weather was mainly good, a calm sea and light breeze, and the clerk was kept busy writing down all his captain's observations as the ship passed islands, bays, points and breakers, of which a special note was made for future reference lest they indicated a reef.

They sailed slowly past Mindoro, hauling up every night, and then on to Panay and Negros. Whilst off Panay, a village and some fishing boats signalled the first signs of human life they had seen and Captain Dethick commented that it was 'very pleasant near the shore and seems to be well cultivated', but all hopes of the smooth passage continuing were soon dashed as a gale suddenly blew up and, catching the ship under full sail, snapped the top of the fore-mast and carried away the cross-tree. The *Griffin* was forced to haul up, but soon the *Oxford*'s carpenter was on board helping to fix some new spars, whilst the *Valentine*'s man was preparing a new section of mast from a spare kept on board his ship. Next day the gale continued unabated and it was all they could do to lash the new mast against the side of the ship but, although there was some rain on the following day, the 19th, the carpenters managed to winch up the new pieces and spent the entire day fitting them into place. By this time the ships were off Mindanao.

The 20th of January dawned with clear skies and a pleasant breeze made for perfect sailing conditions. The day went by without event as they sailed on past the southern tip of Mindanao and into the Sulu Sea. The Hare's Ears were the last major landmark before arriving at Sulu Island; these had been visible for most of the day and, soon after darkness fell, were due east as the fleet passed by. Just over an hour later the *Griffin* was preparing to anchor for the night when disaster struck.

The only people who had any sleep that night were the *Cuddalore*'s sailors: she was lying at anchor on the other side of the island, blissfully unaware of the tragedy unfolding four or five miles to the west. Most of the *Griffin*'s officers and crew crowded into the *Pocock* for the next two days until arrival at Sulu meant they could be redistributed among the remaining four ships. Captain Dethick and Mr Lockwood transferred on to the *Valentine* and everyone else fitted in where they could. Some ships were undermanned and so fifty-four of the sailors and petty officers were able to sign on to their musters, but the remaining twenty-one could not be employed and would therefore receive no wages for this voyage.

Thomas Dethick was both furious and despondent. He was the

commodore of this fleet, but had no command; he was a man used to positions of authority, but was now no more than a passenger receiving polite courtesies befitting his rank. Almost worse was having to speak to his sailors, at least they did not blame him for the loss, but, as eighteen months' work would result in no wages, they could not help being resentful. Thomas Dethick and the other officers had lost nearly £10,000 in the *Griffin*'s wreck. Thomas Lockwood had managed to take one box of valuables off the ship, but had also lost a fortune and, what made matters worse, had resigned his position. At least Dethick still had his captaincy, or so he hoped, assuming the inquiry found him innocent.

They eventually returned to England in September, having had an uneventful passage from Sulu. The Company acted quickly, passing the inquiry on to the Committee of Private Trade, which called all the officers to give evidence at the beginning of October, before they slipped away to the country. On 7 October its findings were reported in the Court minute book: 'Resolved that for the reasons therein mentioned neither Captain Thomas Dethick or his officers are in any way blameworthy with respect to the loss of the ship *Griffin* in the China Sea.'

Under the hereditary bottom convention this meant that the *Griffin* could be replaced with a new ship and work was soon underway. Her old owners, Thomas Hunt and Joseph Salvador, had sold their interest to two new investors, John and Charles Raymond, who became, ten years later, the largest owners of East Indiamen, possessing twenty-nine ships between 1761 and 1780. Thomas Dethick was made captain of a new ship, the *Talbot*, and sailed for Bombay, Mocha and China in 1763.

Dethick had met Elizabeth Arden during the *Griffin*'s stay at Bombay in 1759 and married her there on 25 October 1763. He sailed away again to China and, when he returned to England, resigned from the service on 2 March 1767. It is not at all clear whether he then took passage on an Indiaman and sailed to Bombay in order to bring his wife home, or whether she sailed (with their baby son, Thomas, of whom Dethick knew nothing) separately. Whatever the arrangement, they sold his house in Holborn, London, and retired to Bridgnorth in Shropshire, where he died in 1773. Elizabeth outlived him by fifty years, dying, aged ninety-two, at Pattingham in Staffordshire.

Charles Hudson, by this time a baronet, succeeded to the command of the *Talbot*, but he also died in 1773 after only one voyage.

Dethick's brother-in-law, Samuel Statham, also went to the *Talbot* as purser and had two further voyages before retiring in 1770.

Henry Littleton served under Dethick again in the *Talbot* as third mate but ran on 6 October 1764, whilst the ship was in Bombay.

The *Griffin*'s second mate, David Saunders, went on to become captain of the *Grosvenor* in 1775. This ship, under a different commander, was later wrecked on the western coast of South Africa and became one of the most celebrated disasters of her time, when virtually all the survivors were massacred by the natives *en route* to Cape Town.

The *Griffin*'s old third mate, James Swithin, also became a captain, commanding the *Britannia* from 1771, whilst her fourth mate, Fryer Todd, who had now survived two shipwrecks, served on several other ships and ended up as second mate of the *Royal Captain*, which also sank in the Philippines, though not with him on board.

The 'young gentlemen' who sailed as seamen on the *Griffin* also did well. John Barfoot became chief mate of the *Triton* in 1776 and later commanded an ordinance supply ship. Richard Liell would have become a captain and then joined his family business if he had not died whilst chief mate of the *Stafford* in 1770, and Thomas Eaden eventually became second mate of the *Ponsborne* in 1765.

What happened to the *Griffin* once she sank? Where did all the cargo go? These are the two questions which we must have asked a thousand times during the fourteen months between June 1986 and August 1987. At present these problems are still unsolved. We followed the track of the lost ship from about two miles south of Griffin Rocks for over a mile until the hull finally came to light and, in the course of so doing, uncovered about one-third of her cargo of porcelain. She had left Canton with 125,000 pieces on board; our excavation accounted for only 40,000, so somewhere there are in the region of 85,000 pieces worth perhaps £5 million.

If the chart that the third mate, James Swithin, prepared for the Company's chairman is correct, and Franck believes this to be the case, the ship freed herself of the reef and lay at anchor for a short time before drifting with the current and sinking somewhere close to the spot where we first uncovered her trail. There is a great deal to support this theory as our inspection of the reef revealed nothing; the contemporary report in the newspaper seems to confirm it and we did, after all, find the hull a long way from the reef. It is difficult to imagine that a vessel of 135' could sink on a reef and be propelled underwater as far as three miles, even with a current as strong as five or six knots, so we began the expedition on the basis that the *Griffin* did sink some distance from the rocks, pushed south once the track had been located and did find what we came for. We did not, of course, find all of the ship, nor were we fortunate enough to discover one like the *Geldermalsen*, which appears to have bounced off a reef, sailed a short distance and then sank into a muddy bottom which both held her intact and preserved the cargo. Our ship had lost her stern and her sides, and her cargo was deposited all over the ocean floor.

But was it? The chests containing porcelain were all stowed away in the hold before any tea arrived and lay immediately on top of the ballast which, on 8 October, the day before the first shipment of porcelain arrived, had been levelled throughout the ship about 4" above her keelson so that the draught was 11'10". From the log-books of the *Griffin*'s previous voyages we knew that she had required several alterations in the ballast distribution to keep the bow higher, so it seems clear, both from this fact and other contemporary records of the way porcelain was stored that much more was stacked in the stern section than elsewhere. It stands to reason that, although there was a greater proportion of porcelain found around the hull than anywhere else along the trail, there would have been a great deal more had the stern come away from the ship once she reached her present position. Acting on the premise that it had, we exposed an area up to over one hundred metres south of the hull, expecting to find, at the very least, some trace of the stern and a further quantity of porcelain which, as it had not dropped out when the ship split apart, must have fallen out as it disintegrated. We found nothing at all. No timbers, no ballast bars and only a few plates which could easily have been swept there by the current.

This and several other factors have led Kris to believe that the stern may well have come away before we picked up the trail. An examination of the scatter pattern of ballast bars reveals, at first glance, four major areas where the bars are piled up in quantity and, after each of these deposits, just a light sprinkling until the next concentration. A closer inspection using calipers shows that the distance between most of the pieces of ballast is 30 m, virtually exactly the same length as the section of hull we found. There were also far fewer ballast bars than the twenty to thirty tons which the ship carried. It now seems possible that the ship had left most of her cargo elsewhere and, instead of being pushed bow first, she may have rolled over and over whilst being turned as the current changed direction. If she was open at both ends, like a giant cylinder, the remaining contents would have spilled out every time a new direction was forced or when the current slackened. The spread of the ballast bars by themselves is perhaps not an important discovery, but it does add weight to the possibility that the stern had broken off earlier. This would have also hastened the break-up of the ship and explains why there were no timbers to the south of the hull but a large number to the north. From the spot where the two cases were found to the hull's final resting place, twenty-five metres away, the last vestiges of the sides came away and these two cases were thrown out as the current picked up the nearly flat hull and moved it on again.

This does not provide the answer as to how two cases could survive almost intact after having been thrown around in the hull, nor can we understand why no other timbers were found until the very end except by saying that all the others were carried away by the current. If our hypothesis is correct, and the ship was slowly breaking up all the way along the track, it does explain why there were so many broken pieces of porcelain and the timbers found in one concentrated area were the largest in the ship, and could have been rendered immovable when the current suddenly dropped and deposited all the sand it was carrying, as it often does today. Generally, however, these problems have no explanation until the stern is found and the final sequence of events can be pieced together.

It is possible that the missing porcelain and ballast bars are scattered over an area too large to make further salvage viable, which is the view held by one very experienced diver who has worked on a number of wrecks. It is also possible that the stern, the cannons and all the remaining porcelain lie closer to the reef. 85,000 pieces of porcelain is a lot to go missing, even if they are under fifteen feet of sand, and Kris believes that a good proportion of this was dumped out in one area. At the moment nobody knows where this is or even if it is there at all, but one day Kris Shaffer, Terry Restall and Franck Goddio will go back and find it, and solve the riddle of the *Griffin*.

Appendix

Griffin's Crew List

Name	Rank	Date joined ship (1759)	Entry Log	RB1	RB2	Signing on fee	Monthly wage	Power of attorney to*	Comments
Thomas Dethick	Capt.	5/4	Yes	Yes	Yes	£20	£10	W. Downes	Returned on the *Valentine*.
Charles Hudson	Chief Mate	23/3	Yes	Yes	Yes	£10	£5	Wm. Barnes	
David Saunders	2nd Mate	9/4	Yes	Yes	Yes	£8	£4	John Green	Signed on the *Suffolk*.
James Swithin	3rd Mate	4/4	Yes	Yes	Yes	£7	£3/10/-	Rebekah Swithin	
Fryer Todd	4th Mate	29/3	Yes	Yes	Yes	£5	£2/10/-	Edward Ward	Signed on the *Suffolk*.
Henry Littleton	5th Mate	19/3	Yes	Yes	Yes	£4/10/-			RB2 marked: No. Att. Possibly not on board.
John McFarquhar	Surgeon	5/4	Yes	Yes	Yes	£6/10/-	£3/5/-	Katherine Harvey	Signed on the *Pocock*.
Samuel Statham	Purser	21/3	Yes	Yes	Yes	£4	£2	W. Downes	
Thomas Hodgson	Capt. Clerk	5/4	Yes	Yes	Yes	£4/10/-	£2/5/-	Thos. Bowers	Signed on the *Suffolk*.
Thomas Barnes	Surg. Mate	30/3	Yes	Yes	Yes	£4/10/-	/2/5/-	Geo. Humphreys	Signed on the *Valentine*.
John Wyllie	Gunner	2/4	Yes	Yes	Yes	£7	£3/10/-	Wm. Bland	Sailed on 1755-7 voyage. Signed on the *Valentine*.
Thomas Cock	Carpenter	2/4	Yes	Yes	Yes	£9	£4/10/-	Ann Cock	Sailed on 1755-7 voyage. Signed on the *Valentine*.
Richard Camm	Midshipman	26/3	Yes	Yes	Yes	£4/10/-	£2/5/-	Elizabeth Camm	Signed on the *Valentine*.

Name	Rank	Date				£	£		Notes
James Cowherd	Midshipman	20/3	Yes	Yes	Yes	£4/10/-	£2/5/-	John Brooker	Signed on the *Oxford*.
William Hunt	Midshipman	20/3	Yes	No	Yes	£4/10/-	£2/5/-	Thos. Hunt	
William Corboyde	Coxwain/Midshipman	26/3	Yes	Yes	Yes	£4/10/-	£2/5/-	James & Ann Carter	Small letter in RB2.
Edward Lewis	Boatswain	26/3	Yes	Yes	Yes	£7	£3/10/-	May Lewis	Signed on the *Oxford*.
Andrew Dunn	Quartermaster	27/3	Yes	Yes	Yes	£5	£2/10/-	Ann Jones	Signed on the *Oxford*.
Samuel Jones^x	Quartermaster	27/3	Yes	Yes	Yes	£5	£2/10/-	Frances Jones	
James Scott	Quartermaster	19/3	Yes	Yes	Yes	£5	£2/10/-	– Robinson^x	Signed on the *Suffolk*.
Thomas Thompson	Quartermaster	19/3	Yes	Yes	Yes	£5	£2/10/-	Charles Cooper	Signed on the *Valentine*. Transferred to HMS *Portland* at St Helena.
Charles Butcher	Cooper	20/3	Yes	Yes	Yes	£6	£3	Ralph Sherwood	Sailed on 1755-7 voyage. Signed on the *Valentine*.
William Miller	Ship's Cook	21/3	Yes	Yes	Yes	£5	£2/10/-	Benj. Roads	Signed on the *Suffolk*.
Clement Robinson^x	Ship's Cook	21/3	Yes	Yes	Yes	£5	£2/10/-	Edward Wallis	
Richard Davis	Caulker	26/3	Yes	Yes	Yes	£7/10/-	£3/15/-	John Pelt	Signed on the *Suffolk*.
John Corbett	Carp. 1st Mate	28/3	Yes	Yes	Yes	£6/10/-	£3/5/-	Geo. Colson Smith	Signed on the *Oxford*. Transferred to *Pocock*.
John Wood	Carp. 2nd Mate	26/3	Yes	Yes	Yes	£5	£2/10/-	David Creighton	Sailed on 1755-7 voyage. Signed on the *Oxford*.
Thomas Clifford	Armourer	26/3	Yes	Yes	Yes	£5	£2/10/-	John Mill	RB2 marked: Prest.
Samuel Reeve(s)	Coopers Mate	26/3	Yes	Yes	Yes	£5	£2/10/-	Thos. Podmore	Signed on the *Suffolk*.
Phillip Howell	Gunr. Mate	28/3	Yes	Yes	Yes	£5	£2/10/-	Richard Powell	Signed on the *Valentine*.

Name	Rank	Date joined ship (1759)	Entry			Signing on fee	Monthly wage	Power of attorney to*	Comments
			Log	RB1	RB2				
John Read	Ship's Steward	2/4	Yes	Yes	Yes	£5	£2/10/-	Margaret Read X	Sailed on 1753–5 and 1755–7 voyages. Signed on *Pocock*. Died at St Helena.
Thomas Godfrey	Capt. Steward	5/4	Yes	Yes	Yes	£4	£2	W. Downes	Sailed on 1753–5 and 1755–7 voyages. Died 11 July 1760.
William Farmer	Poulterer	20/3	Yes	Yes	Yes	£4	£2	Henry Baghole	Signed on the *Valentine*.
William Tongue	Barber	26/3	Yes	Yes	Yes	£4	£2	Thos. Tongue	Signed on the *Suffolk*.
John Hill	Butcher	26/3	Yes	Yes	Yes	£4	£2		Signed on the *Valentine*. Transferred to HMS *Portland* at St Helena.
Christian Christianson	Bo's'un Mate	26/3	Yes	No	Yes		£2/10/-	Thos Carr	Signed on the *Valentine*. Transferred to HMS *Portland* at St Helena.
John Dupree	Capt. Cook	29/3	Yes	Yes	Yes	£6/10/-	£3/5/-	Sarah Dupree	Signed on the *Suffolk*.
William Anderson	Baker		Yes	No	Yes		£2/5/-	Himself	RB2 contains letter dated 9/9/1763. Signed on the *Valentine*. Transferred to HMS *Portland* at St Helena.
John Goddard	Capt. Servant	5/4	Yes	Yes	Yes	£2/10/-	£1/5/-	W. Downes	
Thomas Maplesden	Capt. Servant	5/4	Yes	Yes	Yes	£2/10/-	£1/5/-	W. Downes	
John Lloyd	Chief Mate's Servt.	23/3	Yes	Yes	Yes	£2	£1	Wm. Barnes	

Name	Rank	Date				Wage	Next of kin		Notes
George Tilsby	2nd Mate's Servt.	9/4	Yes	Yes	Yes	£1/16/-	John Greene	18/-	Signed on the *Suffolk*.
Andrew Todd	Surg. Servt.		Yes	No	Yes		Katherine Harvey	15/-	Signed on the *Pocock*. Brother of 4th Mate.
John Lancaster Hill	Gunr. Servt.	2/4	Yes	Yes	Yes	£1/10/-	William Bland	15/-	
John Banton	Bo's'un Servt.		Yes	No	No				Drowned 5 Aug. 1759.
George Davis	Carp. Servt.	2/4	Yes	Yes	Yes	£1/10/-	Ann Lock	15/-	Died 13 Nov. 1759.
Thomas Oldfield	Capt. Tailor		No	Yes	Yes	£4		£2	
John Adams	Seaman	19/3	Yes	Yes	Yes	£4/10/-	Johannes Scheelhase	£2/5/-	Signed on the *Valentine*.
John Barfoot	Seaman	23/3	Yes	Yes	Yes	£4/10/-	Wm. Barnes	£2/5/-	
William Barnes	Seaman	27/3	Yes	Yes	Yes	£4/10/-	Thos. Carr	£2/5/-	
Thomas Bastion	Seaman	3/4	Yes	Yes	Yes	£4/10/-	Mary Bastion[x]	£2/5/-	or John.
Harman Behrns	Seaman	19/3	Yes	Yes	Yes	£4/10/-	Johannes Scheelhase	£2/5/-	Signed on the *Oxford* or Barens.
James Bell	Seaman	19/3	Yes	Yes	Yes	£4/10/-	John Dunlop	£2/5/-	Signed on the *Oxford*.
John Bell[x]	Seaman	19/3	Yes	Yes	Yes	£4/10/-	Thos. Buzzard	£2/5/-	Signed on the *Oxford*. Transferred to the *Valentine* at St Helena.
Richard Bennett	Seaman	27/3	Yes	Yes	Yes	£4/10/-	Thos. Carr	£2/5/-	Died 28 Mar. 1760.
Richard Brown	Seaman	20/3	Yes	Yes	Yes	£4/10/-	Wm. Brown	£2/5/-	
Thomas Burrows	Seaman	20/3	Yes	Yes	Yes	£4/10/-	Mary Burrows	£2/5/-	Signed on the *Valentine*. Transferred to HMS *Portland* at St Helena.
Powell Carrol	Seaman	30/3	Yes	Yes	Yes	£4/10/-	–Johnson & Geo Wilson	£2/5/-	Signed on the *Suffolk*.

Name	Rank	Date joined ship (1759)	Entry			Signing on fee	Monthly wage	Power of attorney to*	Comments
			Log	RB1	RB2				
Thomas Donocho	Seaman	30/3	Yes	Yes	Yes	£4/10/-	£2/5/-	Thos. Dennison	Signed on the *Valentine*.
Thomas Eaden	Seaman	5/4	Yes	Yes	Yes	£4/10/-	£2/5/-	Wm. Downes	D.
John East	Seaman	19/3	Yes	Yes	Yes	£4/10/-	£2/5/-	Hannah Gower	Signed on the *Suffolk*.
Andreas Fuchs^X	Seaman	19/3	Yes	Yes	Yes	£4/10/-	£2/5/-	Johannes Scheelhase	Signed on the *Valentine* as Andrew Fowkes.
George Grant^X	Seaman	19/3	Yes	Yes	Yes	£4/10/-	£2/5/-	David Burnett	Died 19 Sept. 1760.
Robert Griffin	Seaman	27/3	Yes	Yes	Yes	£4/10/-	£2/5/-	Thos. Carr	
James Grigg	Seaman	27/3	Yes	Yes	Yes	£4/10/-	£2/5/-	John & Eleanor Barclay	RB2 marked: Prest.
Thomas Grigg	Seaman	27/3	Yes	Yes	Yes	£4/10/-	£2/5/-	John & Eleanor Barclay	
Charles Harden	Seaman	5/4	Yes	Yes	Yes	£4/10/-	£2/5/-	Wm. Downes	D.
Cornelius Hart	Seaman	20/3	Yes	Yes	Yes	£4/10/-	£2/5/-	William Coleman	
Edward Hugil^X	Seaman	20/3	Yes	Yes	Yes	£4/10/-	£2/5/-	Thomas Davies^X	Drowned 26 Aug. 1959
John Johnson	Seaman	20/3	Yes	Yes	Yes	£4/10/-	£2/5/-	Thos. Haswell	Signed on the *Valentine*. Transferred to HMS *Portland* at St Helena.
John Keen^X	Seaman	20/3	Yes	Yes	Yes	£4/10/-	£2/5/-	Henry Plunkett	Or Cain. Signed on *Suffolk*.
John Keveren	Seaman	20/3	Yes	Yes	Yes	£4/10/-	£2/5/-	Joseph & Martha Wittaker	
Richard Liell	Seaman	5/4	Yes	Yes	Yes	£4/10/-	£2/5/-	Wm. Downes	D.
John Lyell	Seaman	20/3	Yes	Yes	Yes	£4/10/-	£2/5/-	Elisha Shepherd	Signed on the *Suffolk*.

Name	Rank	Date				£4/10/-	£2/5/-		Notes
Peter Marks^X	Seaman	2/4	Yes	Yes	Yes	£4/10/-	£2/5/-	John Liberty^X	RB2 marked: Prest.
Jonas Noshum^X	Seaman	2/4	Yes	Yes	Yes	£4/10/-	£2/5/-	– Monson	RB2 marked: Prest
William Peasant^X	Seaman	26/3	Yes	Yes	Yes	£4/10/-	£2/5/-	Elizabeth Peasant	Signed on the *Oxford*. Transferred to the *Valentine* at St Helena.
Peter Ransell	Seaman	26/3	Yes	Yes	Yes	£4/10/-	£2/5/-	Mathew Johnson	Died 6 Nov. 1759
Joseph Raynes	Seaman	26/3	Yes	No	Yes	£4/10/-	£2/5/-	Self	Signed on the *Valentine*. RB2 contains a letter.
John Revell	Seaman	19/3	Yes	Yes	Yes	£4/10/-	£2/5/-	David Burnett	Drowned 26 Aug. 1759.
John Ross^X	Seaman	29/3	Yes	No	No	£4/10/-	£2/5/-	John Weston^X	
Salvadore Saspass	Seaman	26/11	Yes	No	No	?	?		Joined at Bombay. Signed on the *Oxford*.
John Van Sonderen	Seaman	19/3	Yes	Yes	Yes	£4/10/-	£2/5/-	Johannes Scheelhase	Signed on the *Oxford*.
Bartholemew Sike^X	Seaman	2/4	No	Yes	Yes	£4/10/-	£2/5/-	John Liberty^X	RB2 marked: Prest.
Joseph Thomas	Seaman	27/3	Yes	Yes	Yes	£4/10/-	£2/5/-	Richard Powell	RB2 marked: Prest.
John White	Seaman	19/3	Yes	Yes	Yes	£4/10/-	£2/5/-	John Dunlop	Signed on the *Oxford*. Transferred to the *Valentine* at St Helena.
Martin White^X	Seaman	20/3	Yes	Yes	Yes	£4/10/-	£2/5/-	William Coleman^X	Signed on the *Oxford*.
William Whitehead	Seaman	20/3	No	Yes	Yes	£4/10/-	£2/5/-	Samuel Earle	
John Wilson^X	Seaman	19/3	Yes	Yes	Yes	£4/10/-	£2/5/-	John Dunlop	Signed on the *Valentine*. Transferred to HMS *Portland* at St Helena.

Name	Rank	Date joined ship (1759)	Entry Log	RB1	RB2	Signing on fee	Monthly wage	Power of attorney to*	Comments
John Wolf^x	Seaman	2/4	Yes	Yes	Yes	£4/10/-	£2/5/-	John Schroder	RB2 marked: Prest.
Richard Barker	Seaman 2	30/3	Yes	Yes	Yes	£4	£2	Edward Ushor	Died 11 Aug. 1760.
George Brimner	Seaman 2	20/3	Yes	Yes	Yes	£4	£2	Owen & Elizabeth Dayly	Died 10 Dec. 1759.
Henry Brown^x	Seaman 2	26/3	Yes	Yes	Yes	£4	£2	James Love	Signed on the *Suffolk*.
John Cleghorn	Seaman 2	3/4	Yes	Yes	Yes	£4	£2	William Dervar	RB2 marked: Prest.
William Dupree	Seaman 2	29/3	Yes	Yes	Yes	£4	£2	Sarah Dupree	Brother of Captain's cook. Signed on the *Suffolk*.
George Green	Seaman 2	2/4	Yes	Yes	Yes	£4	£2	Charles Langham	RB2 marked: Prest.
Roger Hicks	Seaman 2	27/3	Yes	Yes	Yes	£4	£2		Signed on the *Pocock*.
Joseph James	Seaman 2	27/3	Yes	Yes	Yes	£4	£2	Nathnl. Sterling	Signed on the *Oxford*.
John Prevost^x	Seaman 2	21/3	Yes	Yes	Yes	£4	£2	Ann Murphy	Sailed on the 1755–57 voyage.
William Towers^x	Seaman 2	19/3	Yes	Yes	Yes	£4	£2	Thos. Carr	RB2 marked: Prest.
Thomas Williamson^x	Seaman 2	2/4	Yes	Yes	No	£4	£2		Did not sail. Log says discharged at Spithead 23 Apr. 1759.
Bud Foot	Unknown		Yes	No	Yes	£4	£2		RB2 marked: Prest.
John Morgan	Midshipman ?		Yes	No	Yes		£1/15/-	Mary Morgan	Signed on *Suffolk* as Midshipman.
Christian Fred. Spend	Unknown	19/3	Yes	Yes	Yes	£3/10/-	£1/15/-	Hannah Grouter	Signed on the *Oxford*. Transferred to *Valentine* at St Helena.

The following names appear in various places, however it is considered unlikely that they were on board the Griffin when she sailed for Bombay on 28 April 1759

Name		Date				Amount	Notes
John Beal	?		Yes	No	No		
James Brown	?	20/3	No	Yes	No	£4/10/-	
Martin Brown	?	20/3	No	Yes	No	£4/10/-	
John Cattel	Bo's un Servt.	26/3	No	Yes	No	£1/10/-	
Richard Church	?	20/3	No	Yes	No	£4	
Benjamin Clapp	?	20/3	No	Yes	No	£4/10/-	
George Colley	?	4/4	No	Yes	No	£4	
Hugh Coulter	Sailmaker	28/3	No	Yes	No	£5	
John Van Doreen×	?	19/3	No	Yes	No	£4/10/-	
Barth Leage	?		Yes	No	No		
James Lynch×	?	20/3	No	Yes	No	£4/10/-	
Phillip Mathews	?	2/4	No	Yes	No	£4/10/-	
John Robinson	?	30/3	No	Yes	No	£4	RB1 says: No Attd.
John Salmon	Bo's un Servt.		No	No	Yes	15/-	RB2: name only.
Richard Yarnell	?		Yes	No	No		No entry other than log crew list.

Key and notes

* Power of attorney was given by each man to someone who could claim one month's salary for each six months during the ship's absence. Most men had this paid to a member of their family; however, recurring names indicate that several officers and foreign seamen used professional agents.

Prest. Impressed into service with the Royal Navy in India. The log shows 11 men 'prest'; however HMS *Yarmouth* notes 14 men taken from the *Griffin* on 8 February 1760.

RB1 Receipt Book 1. Signed by each man at the voyage's commencement, this book records signing on fee (equivalent to two months' wages) and imprest money given to the sailors shortly before the ship's departure.

RB2   Receipt Book 2. Completed at the voyage's conclusion, a record of monies due to the sailors with deductions noted by the purser. Sailors who considered they were owed more wrote letters which are found in this book.

X   Illiterate.

D   Signed on board by Captain Dethick. It seems that all those who gave their power of attorney to William Downes were involved with Dethick in some way, or were young gentlemen on their first voyage and being sponsored by Dethick to go as ordinary seamen rather than the more usual practice of signing them on as 'Captain's Servant'.

It seems most likely that 102 Officers and men were on board the *Griffin* when she sailed from England. In India at least 11 and possibly 14 were 'prest' (see note) and 1 was added making either 89 or 92. 10 died during the voyage, so the ship had 79 or 82 on board when she left Canton in January 1761. After the wreck, 57 men are recorded as having signed on to the four remaining Indiamen; one of these died in St Helena and the remainder would have received their full wages for the voyage. Of the officers, all save Dethick, Hudson and Swithin (who may have gone on board the *Cuddalore* with Dalrymple as he published a book in 1762 which relates to orthography of an area where the Indiamen did not sail) found employment. This leaves 19 or 22 men who were probably on board when the *Griffin* sank and could not be used on any of the ships and therefore received no wages. Apparently, either 70 or 73 survivors returned safely to England in September 1761 and it is unknown how many of the men who joined HMS *Portland* at St Helena ever returned home.

Bibliography

Alves, Capt. Walter, *Journal of the Ship London Oct. 1764*, pub. Alexander Dalrymple 1781.

Bedford, John (designer), *Williams Deacons 1771–1970*, pub. 1971.

Birdwood, Sir George, *Report on the Old Records of the India Office*, W.H. Allen 1891.

Blankley, Thomas, *A Naval Expositor*, 1760; reprinted Jean Boudriot 1988.

Bontekoe, Willem, *Memorable Description of the East Indian Voyage 1618–25*, translation George Routledge 1929.

Campbell, John, *Naval History of Great Britain*, 8 vols., London 1813.

Chatterton, E. Keble, *The Old East Indiamen*, Conway Maritime Press reprint 1970.

Coates, Austin, *Macao and the British*, OUP reprint 1988.

Coleman, D.C., *Sir John Banks*, OUP 1963.

Conner, Patrick, *The China Trade*, exhibition catalogue, the Royal Pavilion, Brighton 1986.

Cotton, Sir Evan, (ed.) Sir Charles Fawcett, *East Indiamen*, Batchworth Press 1949.

Dalrymple, Alexander, *Journal of the Schooner Cuddalore: Feb–April 1761*.

Dalrymple, Alexander, *Collection of Charts and Memoirs*, 1772.

Davey, Peter (ed.), *Pipes and Kilns in the London Region*, British Archaeological Reports Series 97, 1981.

Davis, Ralph, *The Rise of the English Shipping Industry*, David & Charles 2nd ed. 1972.

Embree, Ainslie, *Charles Grant and British Rule in India*, Allen & Unwin 1962.

Fortune, Robert, *Three Years Wanderings in China*, Mildmay Books reprint 1987.

Foster, Sir William, *John Company*, John Lane, Bodley Head 1926.

Foster, Sir William, *The English Factories in India 1618–21*, OUP 1906.

Fry, Howard, *Alexander Dalrymple 1737–1808 and the Expansion of British Trade*, Royal Commonwealth Society Imperial Studies Series 29, 1970.

Furber, Holden, *John Company at Work*, Octagon Books NY 1970.

167

Gardner, Brian, *The East India Company*, Hart-Davis 1971.

The Gentleman's Magazine, various dates for Dethick and Hudson families.

Gill, Conrad, *Merchants and Mariners of the Eighteenth Century*, Edward Arnold 1961.

Godden, Geoffrey A., *Oriental Export Market Porcelain*, Granada 1979.

Green, Henry and Robert Wigram, *Chronicles of Blackwall Yard*, 1881.

Hardy, Charles, *A Register of Ships Employed in the Service of the H.E.I.C.*, London 1835.

Heaps, Leo, *Log of the Centurion*, Macmillan 1973.

Howarth, David, *Sovereign of the Seas*, Collins 1974.

Hydrographer of the Navy (pub.), *Philippine Islands Pilot*, 1978.

Hydrographer of the Navy (pub.), *China Sea Pilot* (vol. II), revised 1982.

James, William, *The Naval History of Great Britain*, 6 vols, Richard Bentley 1847.

Jorg, Christiaan, *The Geldermalsen, History and Porcelain*, Kemper (Groningen) 1986.

Lavery, Brian (ed.), *Deane's Doctrine of Naval Architecture 1670*, Conway Maritime Press 1981.

Lloyd, Christopher, *The British Seaman*, Collins 1968.

Lloyds List, various dates 1748–61 including 1 Sept. 1761.

Lubbock, Basil (ed.), *Barlow's Journal*, 2 vols, Hurst & Blackett 1934.

Marsden, Peter, *The Wreck of the Amsterdam*, Hutchinson 1974.

Mathew, K. M., *History of the Portuguese Navigation in India*, Mittal Publications, Delhi 1988.

McGregor, John, *Commercial Statistics*, vol. IV (India), Whittaker & Co. 1850.

Merson, John, *Roads to Xanadu*, Child & Associates & ABC Enterprises, Sydney 1989.

Miller, Russell, *The East Indiamen*, Time Life Books, 4th ed. 1985.

Mottram, R.H., *Traders' Dream, The Romance of the East India Company*, Appleton-Century Co. NY 1939.

Morse, Hosea B., *The Trade and Administration of China*, Longmans, Green & Co. 1913.

Morse, Hosea B., *Chronicles of the East India Company Trading to China*, 5 vols, OUP 1926–9.

Mukherjee, Ramkrishna, *The Rise and Fall of the East India Company*, Monthly Review Press NY 1974.

Oswald, A.H., *New Light on Some Eighteenth Century Pipemakers of London*, 1978.

Parkinson, C. Northcote, *Trade in the Eastern Seas 1793–1813*, Cambridge 1937.

Rediker, Marcus, *Between the Devil and the Deep Blue Sea*, Cambridge

1987.

Rodger, N. A. M., *The Wooden World*, Collins 1986.

Sainsbury, W. Noel (ed.), *Calendar of State Papers* (Colonial) East Indies vol. I, Longman & Roberts 1862.

Sinha, N.N. (ed.), *Fort William – India House Correspondence*, Indian Records Series, Delhi 1957.

Spencer, Alfred (ed.), *The Memoirs of William Hickey*, Hurst & Blackett, 4 vols 1913.

Sutherland, Lucy S., *A London Merchant 1695–1774*, OUP 1933.

Sutton, Jean, *Lords of the East*, Conway Maritime Press, 1981.

Swithin, James, *The Orthography of the Passage from Cape Boliano*, 1762.

Tarling, Nicholas, *Sulu and Sabah*, OUP 1978.

Vollmer, John E., E.J. Keall and E. Nagai-Berthrong, *Silk Roads: China Ships*, exhibition catalogue, Royal Ontario Museum 1983.

Watt, J, Freeman, E. J., and Bynum W. F., *Starving Sailors*, NMM 1981.

Wheatley, Henry (ed.), *The Diary of Samuel Pepys*, 9 vols, George Bell 1899.

Wilbur, Marguerite, *The East India Co*, Richard Smith NY 1945.

Woodruff, Philip, *The Men Who Ruled India*, 2 vols, Jonathan Cape, reprint 1971.

Original sources

India Office Library and Records

Ships

L/Mar/B/603A-D	*Griffin*'s Log Books 1748–1761
L/Mar/B/474A	Log of the *Talbot* (first voyage)
L/Mar/B/397E & F	Log of the *Suffolk*
L/Mar/B/452A	Log of the *Valentine*
L/Mar/B/498A	Log of the *Pocock*
L/Mar/B/588D	Log of the *Oxford*
L/Mar/C/529	Ships 1757–1827 folio 68 is a letter written on board the *Griffin* 14 Nov. 1755.
L/Mar/C/324	Letters to commanders 1716–1814.
L/Mar/C/651	Register of commanders 1737–1832.
L/Mar/C/652	List of officers.

Court Minute Books (B. Series). These run from 1 April to 31 March each year. B77 covers the period April 1761 to March 1762. pp 167–8 contain the report of the Inquiry into the *Griffin*'s loss (7 Oct. 1761).

They also contain the details of ships being tendered and swearing in of officers. To trace the *Griffin*'s officers' careers, Court Minute Books for approximately 40 years were searched.

Correspondence Reports (D. Series)
D/22 Nov 1756 – Jan 1761 f. 78V, 79V, 99V.
D/23 1761–1763 f. 45V, 57V, 66V.

Account Generals Department (L/AG/1/1/). Separate entries exist for Personal Ledgers, Private Trade, Chinaware and Drugs. Headings can be found for Thomas Dethick, Charles Hudson, Owners of the *Griffin* and Thomas Lockwood.

E/4/6   Abstracts of Letters Received from the Coast and Bay 1754–1760.
E/4/7   Abstracts of Letters Received from Bengal 1760–1770.
E/3/87   Early Dethick family involvement with the Company. (Also Court Book Vol 23/230.)
E/4/861 & 862   Dispatches to Madras 1754–59 & 1760–74.

China Factory Records Series (R/10)
R/10/4   Diaries of Supracargoes 1755–1760.
R/10/5   Diaries of Supracargoes 1761–1769.

G/4/1   Dalrymple's original translation of Sulu Treaty (Borneo Letters 1648–1814).
G/12/1   China Book.
G/12/18 Misc. Chinese papers 1753–78.

Java Letter Book 1707–1818 (G/21).
Letters from Alexander Roid pp 15–17.
Letter 54 important account of the *Griffin*'s loss.

Home Misc./93 p. 1   Commission to Capt. Thomas Dethick for seizing pirates 21 Nov. 1748.

L/Mil/9/255/15,17   Thomas Huske Dethick appointed Cadet 4 Dec. 1777.

Bombay Church Records   Captain Thomas Dethick m. Elizabeth Arden 20 Oct. 1763.
Bombay Church Records   Thomas, son of Captain Thomas Dethick by his wife Elizabeth, b. 20 Aug. 1764.

Manuscripts
Mss. Eur. D. 675   Remarks in the Britannia East Indiaman bound for Madras and China 1757–59 (John McQueen).
Mss. Eur. D. 1018   Transcript of Evidence during Enquiry into EIC debt 1767.

Photo Eur. 116   Felix Farley's Bristol Journal provides evidence of
                      fatal depths in ships' well and practise of throwing
                      cannons overboard.
Mss. Eur. E55 K134   An account of intercourse between Europe and
                      China, c. 1797.
Micro Reel 682   Memoir of James Molony (life in Macao 1802).
Mss. Eur. C. 266   Owners Instructions for Royal Admiral.
Mss. Eur. D. 562/16   Papers of Sir George Staunton re. China.

Kent County Archives
Letter Books, Banks mss. ship Dethick Ref U234 B1–3.

Essex Records Office
D/D Ru B20 Contract with Perry & Co for the construction of the *Boscawen*
(Braund Papers).

Public Records Office
PROB 8/167 (Stubbs). Will of Thomas Dethick. Wills also exist for other
members of his family.

PCC 551 (Lushington). Will of John Barfoot.

British Library (Manuscript Room)
Dalrymple letters.
Letter from Charles Hudson.
Dethick Mss. Add Mss 19127.
Ship Book Vol II Add Mss 38872.

British Library (Burney Collection)
London *Evening Chronicle* Sept. 24–26 1761, Vols 74–77.
London *Evening Post*, vol. II 426.

Index